TEACHER'S PET PUBLICATIONS

PUZZLE PACK
for
Shiloh

based on the book by
Phyllis Reynolds Naylor

Written by
Mary B. Collins

© 2005 Teacher's Pet Publications
All Rights Reserved

The materials in this packet are copyrighted
by Teacher's Pet Publications, Inc.

These pages may be duplicated by the purchaser
for use in the purchaser's own classroom.

Copying any of these materials and distributing them
for any other purpose is a violation of the copyright laws.

© 2005 Teacher's Pet Publications, Inc.
www.tpet.com

INTRODUCTION
If you already own the LitPlan for this title, this Puzzle Pack will refresh your Unit Resource Materials and Vocabulary Resource Materials sections plus give you additional materials you can substitute into the tests. If you do not already have a complete LitPlan, these pages will give you some supplemental materials to use with your own plan. There are two main groups of materials: one set for unit words (such as characters' names, symbols, places, etc.) and one set for vocabulary words associated with the book.

WORD LIST
There is a word list for both the unit words and the vocabulary words. These lists show you which words are being used in the materials and the clues or definitions being used for those words. You may want to give students a word list with clues/definitions to help them, or you may want students to only have a word list (without clues/definitions) if you want them to work a little harder. Both are available for duplication. The word lists can also be your "calling key" for the bingo games.

FILL IN THE BLANK AND MATCHING
There are 4 each of the fill in the blank and matching worksheets for both the unit and vocabulary words. These pages can be used either as extra worksheets for students or as objective parts of a unit test. They can be done individually if students need extra help or as a whole class activity to review the material covered.

MAGIC SQUARES
The magic squares not only reinforce the material covered but also work on reasoning and math skills. Many teachers have told us that their students really enjoy doing these!

WORD SEARCH PUZZLES
The word search words go in all directions, as indicated on your answer keys. Two of the word search puzzles have the clues listed rather than the words. This makes the puzzle a little more difficult, but it reinforces the material better. Two word search puzzles have words only for students who find the clue puzzles too difficult.

CROSSWORD PUZZLES
Both unit and vocabulary word sections have 4 crossword puzzles.

BINGO CARDS
There are 32 individual bingo cards for the unit words and 32 individual bingo cards for the vocabulary words. You can use your word list as a "call list," calling the words at random and marking them off of your list as you go, or you could use the flash cards by cutting them apart and drawing the words at random from a hat (or box or whatever). To make a better review, you might ask for the definition and spelling of each word as you call it out–or you could call out the definitions and have students tell you the words they need to look for on the puzzle.

JUGGLE LETTERS
The vocabulary juggle letter game is intended to help students learn the spellings of the words. One sheet has the definitions listed on it as an extra help for students who need it or to reinforce the definitions if you choose to do so.

FLASH CARDS
We've included a set of vocabulary flash cards you can duplicate, cut, and fold for your students. Some teachers make a few sets for general use by the class; others make a set for each student. Some teachers duplicate them for each student and have the students cut & fold their own. You can cut out just the words and put them in a hat, have each student pick out one word and write the definition and a sentence for that word. Students then swap words and papers, with the next student adding a sentence of his own under the last one. You can have students swap as many times as you like. Each time the student will read the sentences written prior to his own and then add a sentence. You can cut out the words and definitions separately and play "I Have; Who Has?" Each student in the room draws a word and definition. The first student says, "I have (the name of the word). Who has the definition?" The student with the definition reads it then says, "I have (the name of the vocabulary word she has). Who has the definition?" The round continues until all words and definitions have been given.

Shiloh Word List

No.	Word	Clue/Definition
1.	ALLERGIC	David's Aunt Pat is ___ to dogs
2.	BAKER	Owned the German Shepherd in the book
3.	BEAGLE	Shiloh was this kind of a dog
4.	BECKY	Marty's younger sister
5.	BLOOD	What David saw all over the dog pen
6.	CONTRACT	What Judd signed about the dog
7.	DAVID	Marty's best friend's first name
8.	DEER	Marty saw Judd shoot this animal
9.	ELEVEN	Marty's age
10.	FEEBLE	What Grandma Preston is
11.	HERMIE	Name for David's hermit crab
12.	HOWARD	David's last name
13.	JUDD	The real owner of Shiloh
14.	KITE	David brought this for Marty to play with
15.	LAW	Marty's father said, 'You've got to go by the ___.'
16.	LIES	What Marty told to keep Shiloh
17.	MA	What Marty called his mother
18.	MARTY	Person who worked hard to earn Shiloh
19.	MURPHY	Veterinarian's name: Doc ___
20.	NAYLOR	Author's last name
21.	PEN	What Marty built for the dog
22.	PET	David's hermit crab is his ___
23.	PRESTON	Marty's last name
24.	RAY	Marty's father's first name
25.	SCRAM	What Judd called some of his dogs
26.	SEARS	Store having their catalogues delivered by mail
27.	SHILOH	Name of Marty's new dog
28.	SNAKES	What Marty threatened his sister Dara Lynn with
29.	SQUASH	Food that gave Marty's schemes away
30.	SUNDAY	Day on which SHILOH begins
31.	WALLACE	Grocer's name
32.	WVA	Initials of Marty's home state
33.	YELPS	What Marty and his father heard coming from the dog pen

Shiloh Fill In The Blanks 1

1. Name for David's hermit crab
2. Marty's younger sister
3. David's Aunt Pat is ___ to dogs
4. Shiloh was this kind of a dog
5. Owned the German Shepherd in the book
6. Food that gave Marty's schemes away
7. Name of Marty's new dog
8. Marty's father said, 'You've got to go by the ___.'
9. What Marty and his father heard coming from the dog pen
10. Marty's best friend's first name
11. What Marty built for the dog
12. What Marty told to keep Shiloh
13. Store having their catalogues delivered by mail
14. Veterinarian's name: Doc ___
15. What Marty threatened his sister Dara Lynn with
16. David's last name
17. What David saw all over the dog pen
18. David brought this for Marty to play with
19. Grocer's name
20. David's hermit crab is his ___

Shiloh Fill In The Blanks 1 Answer Key

HERMIE	1. Name for David's hermit crab
BECKY	2. Marty's younger sister
ALLERGIC	3. David's Aunt Pat is ___ to dogs
BEAGLE	4. Shiloh was this kind of a dog
BAKER	5. Owned the German Shepherd in the book
SQUASH	6. Food that gave Marty's schemes away
SHILOH	7. Name of Marty's new dog
LAW	8. Marty's father said, 'You've got to go by the ___.'
YELPS	9. What Marty and his father heard coming from the dog pen
DAVID	10. Marty's best friend's first name
PEN	11. What Marty built for the dog
LIES	12. What Marty told to keep Shiloh
SEARS	13. Store having their catalogues delivered by mail
MURPHY	14. Veterinarian's name: Doc ___
SNAKES	15. What Marty threatened his sister Dara Lynn with
HOWARD	16. David's last name
BLOOD	17. What David saw all over the dog pen
KITE	18. David brought this for Marty to play with
WALLACE	19. Grocer's name
PET	20. David's hermit crab is his ___

Shiloh Fill In The Blanks 2

_____ 1. Marty saw Judd shoot this animal

_____ 2. What Marty threatened his sister Dara Lynn with

_____ 3. What Judd called some of his dogs

_____ 4. Grocer's name

_____ 5. Marty's younger sister

_____ 6. Owned the German Shepherd in the book

_____ 7. What Marty built for the dog

_____ 8. What Judd signed about the dog

_____ 9. David's Aunt Pat is ___ to dogs

_____ 10. Initials of Marty's home state

_____ 11. Marty's father said, 'You've got to go by the ___.'

_____ 12. Store having their catalogues delivered by mail

_____ 13. What Marty told to keep Shiloh

_____ 14. David's last name

_____ 15. Marty's age

_____ 16. Veterinarian's name: Doc ___

_____ 17. Marty's best friend's first name

_____ 18. What Marty and his father heard coming from the dog pen

_____ 19. David brought this for Marty to play with

_____ 20. Food that gave Marty's schemes away

Shiloh Fill In The Blanks 2 Answer Key

DEER		1. Marty saw Judd shoot this animal
SNAKES		2. What Marty threatened his sister Dara Lynn with
SCRAM		3. What Judd called some of his dogs
WALLACE		4. Grocer's name
BECKY		5. Marty's younger sister
BAKER		6. Owned the German Shepherd in the book
PEN		7. What Marty built for the dog
CONTRACT		8. What Judd signed about the dog
ALLERGIC		9. David's Aunt Pat is ___ to dogs
WVA		10. Initials of Marty's home state
LAW		11. Marty's father said, 'You've got to go by the ___.'
SEARS		12. Store having their catalogues delivered by mail
LIES		13. What Marty told to keep Shiloh
HOWARD		14. David's last name
ELEVEN		15. Marty's age
MURPHY		16. Veterinarian's name: Doc ___
DAVID		17. Marty's best friend's first name
YELPS		18. What Marty and his father heard coming from the dog pen
KITE		19. David brought this for Marty to play with
SQUASH		20. Food that gave Marty's schemes away

Shiloh Fill In The Blanks 3

_____ 1. What Marty and his father heard coming from the dog pen
_____ 2. Marty's father said, 'You've got to go by the ___.'
_____ 3. Store having their catalogues delivered by mail
_____ 4. Initials of Marty's home state
_____ 5. What Marty threatened his sister Dara Lynn with
_____ 6. Marty's best friend's first name
_____ 7. David's hermit crab is his ___
_____ 8. Marty's last name
_____ 9. What Marty told to keep Shiloh
_____ 10. The real owner of Shiloh
_____ 11. David's last name
_____ 12. Author's last name
_____ 13. David brought this for Marty to play with
_____ 14. Name for David's hermit crab
_____ 15. Day on which SHILOH begins
_____ 16. What Judd called some of his dogs
_____ 17. What Judd signed about the dog
_____ 18. Marty saw Judd shoot this animal
_____ 19. What David saw all over the dog pen
_____ 20. Food that gave Marty's schemes away

Shiloh Fill In The Blanks 3 Answer Key

Answer	#	Clue
YELPS	1.	What Marty and his father heard coming from the dog pen
LAW	2.	Marty's father said, 'You've got to go by the ___.'
SEARS	3.	Store having their catalogues delivered by mail
WVA	4.	Initials of Marty's home state
SNAKES	5.	What Marty threatened his sister Dara Lynn with
DAVID	6.	Marty's best friend's first name
PET	7.	David's hermit crab is his ___
PRESTON	8.	Marty's last name
LIES	9.	What Marty told to keep Shiloh
JUDD	10.	The real owner of Shiloh
HOWARD	11.	David's last name
NAYLOR	12.	Author's last name
KITE	13.	David brought this for Marty to play with
HERMIE	14.	Name for David's hermit crab
SUNDAY	15.	Day on which SHILOH begins
SCRAM	16.	What Judd called some of his dogs
CONTRACT	17.	What Judd signed about the dog
DEER	18.	Marty saw Judd shoot this animal
BLOOD	19.	What David saw all over the dog pen
SQUASH	20.	Food that gave Marty's schemes away

Shiloh Fill In The Blanks 4

_____ 1. What Marty told to keep Shiloh
_____ 2. David's Aunt Pat is ___ to dogs
_____ 3. Author's last name
_____ 4. Marty's younger sister
_____ 5. Store having their catalogues delivered by mail
_____ 6. The real owner of Shiloh
_____ 7. What Judd signed about the dog
_____ 8. Person who worked hard to earn Shiloh
_____ 9. What David saw all over the dog pen
_____ 10. Day on which SHILOH begins
_____ 11. Name of Marty's new dog
_____ 12. David brought this for Marty to play with
_____ 13. Shiloh was this kind of a dog
_____ 14. Marty's best friend's first name
_____ 15. What Marty built for the dog
_____ 16. What Marty and his father heard coming from the dog pen
_____ 17. Grocer's name
_____ 18. David's hermit crab is his ___
_____ 19. Marty's father's first name
_____ 20. Veterinarian's name: Doc ___

Shiloh Fill In The Blanks 4 Answer Key

LIES	1. What Marty told to keep Shiloh
ALLERGIC	2. David's Aunt Pat is ___ to dogs
NAYLOR	3. Author's last name
BECKY	4. Marty's younger sister
SEARS	5. Store having their catalogues delivered by mail
JUDD	6. The real owner of Shiloh
CONTRACT	7. What Judd signed about the dog
MARTY	8. Person who worked hard to earn Shiloh
BLOOD	9. What David saw all over the dog pen
SUNDAY	10. Day on which SHILOH begins
SHILOH	11. Name of Marty's new dog
KITE	12. David brought this for Marty to play with
BEAGLE	13. Shiloh was this kind of a dog
DAVID	14. Marty's best friend's first name
PEN	15. What Marty built for the dog
YELPS	16. What Marty and his father heard coming from the dog pen
WALLACE	17. Grocer's name
PET	18. David's hermit crab is his ___
RAY	19. Marty's father's first name
MURPHY	20. Veterinarian's name: Doc ___

Shiloh Matching 1

___ 1. BECKY　　　　A. Name for David's hermit crab
___ 2. PEN　　　　　B. What Marty and his father heard coming from the dog pen
___ 3. SHILOH　　　 C. Owned the German Shepherd in the book
___ 4. SNAKES　　　D. Name of Marty's new dog
___ 5. PRESTON　　 E. David's hermit crab is his ___
___ 6. LAW　　　　　F. Store having their catalogues delivered by mail
___ 7. SCRAM　　　 G. Food that gave Marty's schemes away
___ 8. PET　　　　　H. Marty's age
___ 9. SQUASH　　　I. Marty's younger sister
___10. SEARS　　　 J. Grocer's name
___11. CONTRACT　　K. What Judd called some of his dogs
___12. RAY　　　　　L. Veterinarian's name: Doc ___
___13. JUDD　　　　M. What Grandma Preston is
___14. HERMIE　　　N. David brought this for Marty to play with
___15. MA　　　　　 O. Marty's father's first name
___16. MURPHY　　　P. What Marty threatened his sister Dara Lynn with
___17. SUNDAY　　　Q. Shiloh was this kind of a dog
___18. YELPS　　　 R. What Judd signed about the dog
___19. BEAGLE　　　S. Marty's father said, 'You've got to go by the ___.'
___20. WVA　　　　 T. What Marty called his mother
___21. KITE　　　　 U. Marty's last name
___22. BAKER　　　 V. What Marty built for the dog
___23. WALLACE　　 W. Initials of Marty's home state
___24. FEEBLE　　　X. Day on which SHILOH begins
___25. ELEVEN　　　Y. The real owner of Shiloh

Shiloh Matching 1 Answer Key

I -	1. BECKY	A.	Name for David's hermit crab
V -	2. PEN	B.	What Marty and his father heard coming from the dog pen
D -	3. SHILOH	C.	Owned the German Shepherd in the book
P -	4. SNAKES	D.	Name of Marty's new dog
U -	5. PRESTON	E.	David's hermit crab is his ___
S -	6. LAW	F.	Store having their catalogues delivered by mail
K -	7. SCRAM	G.	Food that gave Marty's schemes away
E -	8. PET	H.	Marty's age
G -	9. SQUASH	I.	Marty's younger sister
F -	10. SEARS	J.	Grocer's name
R -	11. CONTRACT	K.	What Judd called some of his dogs
O -	12. RAY	L.	Veterinarian's name: Doc ___
Y -	13. JUDD	M.	What Grandma Preston is
A -	14. HERMIE	N.	David brought this for Marty to play with
T -	15. MA	O.	Marty's father's first name
L -	16. MURPHY	P.	What Marty threatened his sister Dara Lynn with
X -	17. SUNDAY	Q.	Shiloh was this kind of a dog
B -	18. YELPS	R.	What Judd signed about the dog
Q -	19. BEAGLE	S.	Marty's father said, 'You've got to go by the ___.'
W -	20. WVA	T.	What Marty called his mother
N -	21. KITE	U.	Marty's last name
C -	22. BAKER	V.	What Marty built for the dog
J -	23. WALLACE	W.	Initials of Marty's home state
M -	24. FEEBLE	X.	Day on which SHILOH begins
H -	25. ELEVEN	Y.	The real owner of Shiloh

Copyrighted

Shiloh Matching 2

___ 1. BLOOD   A. What Marty threatened his sister Dara Lynn with
___ 2. BEAGLE   B. David brought this for Marty to play with
___ 3. MA   C. What Judd called some of his dogs
___ 4. PEN   D. Marty's younger sister
___ 5. SHILOH   E. Author's last name
___ 6. ALLERGIC   F. Marty's last name
___ 7. SNAKES   G. David's Aunt Pat is ___ to dogs
___ 8. PRESTON   H. Veterinarian's name: Doc ___
___ 9. ELEVEN   I. What Judd signed about the dog
___10. MURPHY   J. Marty's age
___11. WVA   K. What David saw all over the dog pen
___12. BECKY   L. Name of Marty's new dog
___13. NAYLOR   M. What Marty called his mother
___14. KITE   N. David's last name
___15. LAW   O. Initials of Marty's home state
___16. CONTRACT   P. Marty's best friend's first name
___17. SEARS   Q. Name for David's hermit crab
___18. HERMIE   R. Marty's father said, 'You've got to go by the ___.'
___19. SCRAM   S. Shiloh was this kind of a dog
___20. DEER   T. Grocer's name
___21. HOWARD   U. What Marty and his father heard coming from the dog pen
___22. DAVID   V. Marty saw Judd shoot this animal
___23. WALLACE   W. Store having their catalogues delivered by mail
___24. YELPS   X. Food that gave Marty's schemes away
___25. SQUASH   Y. What Marty built for the dog

Shiloh Matching 2 Answer Key

K - 1. BLOOD	A.	What Marty threatened his sister Dara Lynn with
S - 2. BEAGLE	B.	David brought this for Marty to play with
M - 3. MA	C.	What Judd called some of his dogs
Y - 4. PEN	D.	Marty's younger sister
L - 5. SHILOH	E.	Author's last name
G - 6. ALLERGIC	F.	Marty's last name
A - 7. SNAKES	G.	David's Aunt Pat is ___ to dogs
F - 8. PRESTON	H.	Veterinarian's name: Doc ___
J - 9. ELEVEN	I.	What Judd signed about the dog
H -10. MURPHY	J.	Marty's age
O -11. WVA	K.	What David saw all over the dog pen
D -12. BECKY	L.	Name of Marty's new dog
E -13. NAYLOR	M.	What Marty called his mother
B -14. KITE	N.	David's last name
R -15. LAW	O.	Initials of Marty's home state
I - 16. CONTRACT	P.	Marty's best friend's first name
W -17. SEARS	Q.	Name for David's hermit crab
Q -18. HERMIE	R.	Marty's father said, 'You've got to go by the ___.'
C -19. SCRAM	S.	Shiloh was this kind of a dog
V -20. DEER	T.	Grocer's name
N -21. HOWARD	U.	What Marty and his father heard coming from the dog pen
P -22. DAVID	V.	Marty saw Judd shoot this animal
T -23. WALLACE	W.	Store having their catalogues delivered by mail
U -24. YELPS	X.	Food that gave Marty's schemes away
X -25. SQUASH	Y.	What Marty built for the dog

Shiloh Matching 3

___ 1. ELEVEN A. Marty saw Judd shoot this animal
___ 2. FEEBLE B. Day on which SHILOH begins
___ 3. DEER C. What Marty told to keep Shiloh
___ 4. SEARS D. What Marty threatened his sister Dara Lynn with
___ 5. PET E. What Grandma Preston is
___ 6. SHILOH F. Marty's father said, 'You've got to go by the ___.'
___ 7. JUDD G. What Marty called his mother
___ 8. SNAKES H. David's Aunt Pat is ___ to dogs
___ 9. DAVID I. Veterinarian's name: Doc ___
___ 10. BAKER J. David brought this for Marty to play with
___ 11. WALLACE K. Marty's last name
___ 12. HERMIE L. Name of Marty's new dog
___ 13. MA M. Owned the German Shepherd in the book
___ 14. LAW N. Marty's age
___ 15. MURPHY O. The real owner of Shiloh
___ 16. PRESTON P. What Marty built for the dog
___ 17. SQUASH Q. Marty's best friend's first name
___ 18. PEN R. Marty's father's first name
___ 19. CONTRACT S. Name for David's hermit crab
___ 20. ALLERGIC T. Grocer's name
___ 21. SUNDAY U. Shiloh was this kind of a dog
___ 22. LIES V. Food that gave Marty's schemes away
___ 23. KITE W. What Judd signed about the dog
___ 24. RAY X. David's hermit crab is his ___
___ 25. BEAGLE Y. Store having their catalogues delivered by mail

Shiloh Matching 3 Answer Key

N - 1.	ELEVEN	A.	Marty saw Judd shoot this animal
E - 2.	FEEBLE	B.	Day on which SHILOH begins
A - 3.	DEER	C.	What Marty told to keep Shiloh
Y - 4.	SEARS	D.	What Marty threatened his sister Dara Lynn with
X - 5.	PET	E.	What Grandma Preston is
L - 6.	SHILOH	F.	Marty's father said, 'You've got to go by the ___.'
O - 7.	JUDD	G.	What Marty called his mother
D - 8.	SNAKES	H.	David's Aunt Pat is ___ to dogs
Q - 9.	DAVID	I.	Veterinarian's name: Doc ___
M - 10.	BAKER	J.	David brought this for Marty to play with
T - 11.	WALLACE	K.	Marty's last name
S - 12.	HERMIE	L.	Name of Marty's new dog
G - 13.	MA	M.	Owned the German Shepherd in the book
F - 14.	LAW	N.	Marty's age
I - 15.	MURPHY	O.	The real owner of Shiloh
K - 16.	PRESTON	P.	What Marty built for the dog
V - 17.	SQUASH	Q.	Marty's best friend's first name
P - 18.	PEN	R.	Marty's father's first name
W - 19.	CONTRACT	S.	Name for David's hermit crab
H - 20.	ALLERGIC	T.	Grocer's name
B - 21.	SUNDAY	U.	Shiloh was this kind of a dog
C - 22.	LIES	V.	Food that gave Marty's schemes away
J - 23.	KITE	W.	What Judd signed about the dog
R - 24.	RAY	X.	David's hermit crab is his ___
U - 25.	BEAGLE	Y.	Store having their catalogues delivered by mail

Shiloh Matching 4

___ 1. SCRAM   A. What Marty called his mother
___ 2. LAW   B. Marty's age
___ 3. BAKER   C. David's Aunt Pat is ___ to dogs
___ 4. KITE   D. Name for David's hermit crab
___ 5. YELPS   E. David brought this for Marty to play with
___ 6. DEER   F. What Judd called some of his dogs
___ 7. SHILOH   G. What Marty built for the dog
___ 8. MURPHY   H. What Judd signed about the dog
___ 9. ELEVEN   I. Marty's father said, 'You've got to go by the ___.'
___ 10. CONTRACT   J. What Grandma Preston is
___ 11. LIES   K. What Marty told to keep Shiloh
___ 12. HERMIE   L. Grocer's name
___ 13. SQUASH   M. Person who worked hard to earn Shiloh
___ 14. MARTY   N. Store having their catalogues delivered by mail
___ 15. PRESTON   O. Initials of Marty's home state
___ 16. BECKY   P. Veterinarian's name: Doc ___
___ 17. WVA   Q. Marty's last name
___ 18. ALLERGIC   R. Food that gave Marty's schemes away
___ 19. SUNDAY   S. Day on which SHILOH begins
___ 20. FEEBLE   T. Name of Marty's new dog
___ 21. MA   U. Marty's father's first name
___ 22. PEN   V. What Marty and his father heard coming from the dog pen
___ 23. SEARS   W. Marty saw Judd shoot this animal
___ 24. RAY   X. Owned the German Shepherd in the book
___ 25. WALLACE   Y. Marty's younger sister

Shiloh Matching 4 Answer Key

F - 1. SCRAM	A.	What Marty called his mother
I - 2. LAW	B.	Marty's age
X - 3. BAKER	C.	David's Aunt Pat is ___ to dogs
E - 4. KITE	D.	Name for David's hermit crab
V - 5. YELPS	E.	David brought this for Marty to play with
W - 6. DEER	F.	What Judd called some of his dogs
T - 7. SHILOH	G.	What Marty built for the dog
P - 8. MURPHY	H.	What Judd signed about the dog
B - 9. ELEVEN	I.	Marty's father said, 'You've got to go by the ___.'
H - 10. CONTRACT	J.	What Grandma Preston is
K - 11. LIES	K.	What Marty told to keep Shiloh
D - 12. HERMIE	L.	Grocer's name
R - 13. SQUASH	M.	Person who worked hard to earn Shiloh
M - 14. MARTY	N.	Store having their catalogues delivered by mail
Q - 15. PRESTON	O.	Initials of Marty's home state
Y - 16. BECKY	P.	Veterinarian's name: Doc ___
O - 17. WVA	Q.	Marty's last name
C - 18. ALLERGIC	R.	Food that gave Marty's schemes away
S - 19. SUNDAY	S.	Day on which SHILOH begins
J - 20. FEEBLE	T.	Name of Marty's new dog
A - 21. MA	U.	Marty's father's first name
G - 22. PEN	V.	What Marty and his father heard coming from the dog pen
N - 23. SEARS	W.	Marty saw Judd shoot this animal
U - 24. RAY	X.	Owned the German Shepherd in the book
L - 25. WALLACE	Y.	Marty's younger sister

Shiloh Magic Squares 1

Match the definition with the vocabulary word. Put your answers in the magic squares below. When your answers are correct, all columns and rows will add to the same number.

A. CONTRACT   E. BECKY   I. KITE   M. SCRAM
B. SNAKES   F. BEAGLE   J. PET   N. JUDD
C. NAYLOR   G. HERMIE   K. PRESTON   O. WALLACE
D. RAY   H. DAVID   L. FEEBLE   P. BLOOD

1. Author's last name
2. David's hermit crab is his ___
3. Shiloh was this kind of a dog
4. Grocer's name
5. What David saw all over the dog pen
6. Marty's younger sister
7. David brought this for Marty to play with
8. Marty's father's first name
9. What Judd called some of his dogs
10. Marty's best friend's first name
11. What Grandma Preston is
12. What Judd signed about the dog
13. What Marty threatened his sister Dara Lynn with
14. Marty's last name
15. Name for David's hermit crab
16. The real owner of Shiloh

A=	B=	C=	D=
E=	F=	G=	H=
I=	J=	K=	L=
M=	N=	O=	P=

Shiloh Magic Squares 1 Answer Key

Match the definition with the vocabulary word. Put your answers in the magic squares below. When your answers are correct, all columns and rows will add to the same number.

A. CONTRACT E. BECKY   I. KITE   M. SCRAM
B. SNAKES   F. BEAGLE J. PET   N. JUDD
C. NAYLOR   G. HERMIE K. PRESTON   O. WALLACE
D. RAY   H. DAVID   L. FEEBLE   P. BLOOD

1. Author's last name
2. David's hermit crab is his ___
3. Shiloh was this kind of a dog
4. Grocer's name
5. What David saw all over the dog pen
6. Marty's younger sister
7. David brought this for Marty to play with
8. Marty's father's first name
9. What Judd called some of his dogs
10. Marty's best friend's first name
11. What Grandma Preston is
12. What Judd signed about the dog
13. What Marty threatened his sister Dara Lynn with
14. Marty's last name
15. Name for David's hermit crab
16. The real owner of Shiloh

A=12	B=13	C=1	D=8
E=6	F=3	G=15	H=10
I=7	J=2	K=14	L=11
M=9	N=16	O=4	P=5

Shiloh Magic Squares 2

Match the definition with the vocabulary word. Put your answers in the magic squares below. When your answers are correct, all columns and rows will add to the same number.

A. DEER
B. NAYLOR
C. YELPS
D. SNAKES
E. WVA
F. SHILOH
G. SQUASH
H. FEEBLE
I. ELEVEN
J. RAY
K. CONTRACT
L. LIES
M. JUDD
N. PEN
O. BLOOD
P. WALLACE

1. What Grandma Preston is
2. Marty saw Judd shoot this animal
3. Author's last name
4. Food that gave Marty's schemes away
5. Marty's father's first name
6. What David saw all over the dog pen
7. Grocer's name
8. Marty's age
9. What Judd signed about the dog
10. What Marty built for the dog
11. The real owner of Shiloh
12. What Marty told to keep Shiloh
13. Initials of Marty's home state
14. What Marty threatened his sister Dara Lynn with
15. What Marty and his father heard coming from the dog pen
16. Name of Marty's new dog

A=	B=	C=	D=
E=	F=	G=	H=
I=	J=	K=	L=
M=	N=	O=	P=

Shiloh Magic Squares 2 Answer Key

Match the definition with the vocabulary word. Put your answers in the magic squares below. When your answers are correct, all columns and rows will add to the same number.

A. DEER
B. NAYLOR
C. YELPS
D. SNAKES
E. WVA
F. SHILOH
G. SQUASH
H. FEEBLE
I. ELEVEN
J. RAY
K. CONTRACT
L. LIES
M. JUDD
N. PEN
O. BLOOD
P. WALLACE

1. What Grandma Preston is
2. Marty saw Judd shoot this animal
3. Author's last name
4. Food that gave Marty's schemes away
5. Marty's father's first name
6. What David saw all over the dog pen
7. Grocer's name
8. Marty's age
9. What Judd signed about the dog
10. What Marty built for the dog
11. The real owner of Shiloh
12. What Marty told to keep Shiloh
13. Initials of Marty's home state
14. What Marty threatened his sister Dara Lynn with
15. What Marty and his father heard coming from the dog pen
16. Name of Marty's new dog

A=2	B=3	C=15	D=14
E=13	F=16	G=4	H=1
I=8	J=5	K=9	L=12
M=11	N=10	O=6	P=7

Shiloh Magic Squares 3

Match the definition with the vocabulary word. Put your answers in the magic squares below. When your answers are correct, all columns and rows will add to the same number.

A. KITE E. MURPHY I. RAY M. BAKER
B. DAVID F. FEEBLE J. SEARS N. PEN
C. JUDD G. SQUASH K. LAW O. DEER
D. LIES H. CONTRACT L. BECKY P. ELEVEN

1. The real owner of Shiloh
2. Store having their catalogues delivered by mail
3. What Grandma Preston is
4. Marty saw Judd shoot this animal
5. Marty's age
6. Veterinarian's name: Doc ___
7. Marty's father's first name
8. What Marty told to keep Shiloh
9. Owned the German Shepherd in the book
10. What Judd signed about the dog
11. Marty's younger sister
12. David brought this for Marty to play with
13. Marty's best friend's first name
14. Marty's father said, 'You've got to go by the ___.'
15. Food that gave Marty's schemes away
16. What Marty built for the dog

A=	B=	C=	D=
E=	F=	G=	H=
I=	J=	K=	L=
M=	N=	O=	P=

Shiloh Magic Squares 3 Answer Key

Match the definition with the vocabulary word. Put your answers in the magic squares below. When your answers are correct, all columns and rows will add to the same number.

A. KITE
B. DAVID
C. JUDD
D. LIES
E. MURPHY
F. FEEBLE
G. SQUASH
H. CONTRACT
I. RAY
J. SEARS
K. LAW
L. BECKY
M. BAKER
N. PEN
O. DEER
P. ELEVEN

1. The real owner of Shiloh
2. Store having their catalogues delivered by mail
3. What Grandma Preston is
4. Marty saw Judd shoot this animal
5. Marty's age
6. Veterinarian's name: Doc ___
7. Marty's father's first name
8. What Marty told to keep Shiloh
9. Owned the German Shepherd in the book
10. What Judd signed about the dog
11. Marty's younger sister
12. David brought this for Marty to play with
13. Marty's best friend's first name
14. Marty's father said, 'You've got to go by the ___.'
15. Food that gave Marty's schemes away
16. What Marty built for the dog

A=12	B=13	C=1	D=8
E=6	F=3	G=15	H=10
I=7	J=2	K=14	L=11
M=9	N=16	O=4	P=5

Shiloh Magic Squares 4

Match the definition with the vocabulary word. Put your answers in the magic squares below. When your answers are correct, all columns and rows will add to the same number.

A. WALLACE   E. KITE   I. FEEBLE   M. SUNDAY
B. SNAKES   F. MURPHY   J. DEER   N. CONTRACT
C. HERMIE   G. PRESTON   K. SQUASH   O. ELEVEN
D. LAW   H. WVA   L. HOWARD   P. SHILOH

1. What Marty threatened his sister Dara Lynn with
2. Marty's last name
3. Food that gave Marty's schemes away
4. What Judd signed about the dog
5. Day on which SHILOH begins
6. David's last name
7. Initials of Marty's home state
8. Grocer's name
9. Name of Marty's new dog
10. What Grandma Preston is
11. David brought this for Marty to play with
12. Marty's father said, 'You've got to go by the ___.'
13. Name for David's hermit crab
14. Veterinarian's name: Doc ___
15. Marty saw Judd shoot this animal
16. Marty's age

A=	B=	C=	D=
E=	F=	G=	H=
I=	J=	K=	L=
M=	N=	O=	P=

Shiloh Magic Squares 4 Answer Key

Match the definition with the vocabulary word. Put your answers in the magic squares below. When your answers are correct, all columns and rows will add to the same number.

A. WALLACE E. KITE   I. FEEBLE   M. SUNDAY
B. SNAKES   F. MURPHY   J. DEER   N. CONTRACT
C. HERMIE   G. PRESTON   K. SQUASH   O. ELEVEN
D. LAW   H. WVA   L. HOWARD   P. SHILOH

1. What Marty threatened his sister Dara Lynn with
2. Marty's last name
3. Food that gave Marty's schemes away
4. What Judd signed about the dog
5. Day on which SHILOH begins
6. David's last name
7. Initials of Marty's home state
8. Grocer's name
9. Name of Marty's new dog
10. What Grandma Preston is
11. David brought this for Marty to play with
12. Marty's father said, 'You've got to go by the ___.'
13. Name for David's hermit crab
14. Veterinarian's name: Doc ___
15. Marty saw Judd shoot this animal
16. Marty's age

A=8	B=1	C=13	D=12
E=11	F=14	G=2	H=7
I=10	J=15	K=3	L=6
M=5	N=4	O=16	P=9

Shiloh Word Search 1

Words are placed backwards, forward, diagonally, up and down. Clues listed below can help you find the words. Circle the hidden vocabulary words in the maze.

K	D	H	C	R	F	Z	R	Z	S	X	W	Y	B	Y	C	T	Q	K	C
R	J	C	K	T	S	J	G	F	B	J	P	Z	T	T	P	L	F	J	B
F	P	X	D	P	J	J	S	G	D	R	J	X	B	M	W	B	K	J	Q
A	B	C	Y	B	C	W	G	C	W	R	J	K	Q	F	T	L	P	Z	S
L	K	H	J	Y	D	Z	G	H	R	D	R	P	N	J	V	V	R	H	T
L	Y	X	H	V	W	P	M	J	V	G	D	H	R	F	D	D	R	Q	K
E	B	S	M	J	X	P	Q	M	K	D	C	G	C	E	J	F	R	H	W
R	X	E	V	T	Y	M	S	Y	H	W	C	K	F	J	S	K	K	B	L
G	K	K	N	A	J	A	S	P	S	N	W	W	I	C	P	T	A	R	D
I	F	A	D	M	W	R	S	H	L	E	V	W	P	T	L	K	O	S	H
C	O	N	T	R	A	C	T	D	I	V	A	D	E	L	E	V	E	N	N
T	U	S	K	J	N	S	E	N	L	S	L	H	R	T	R	Y	I	I	P	B
S	C	P	B	G	R	E	N	M	L	L	O	D	S	D	L	J	M	J	X
H	X	N	V	R	R	B	Y	A	D	Y	S	H	M	Y	Y	P	R	M	K
O	N	A	Y	L	O	R	C	R	A	Y	X	B	E	A	G	L	E	M	N
W	M	Z	V	C	K	E	J	T	Y	Z	L	E	Z	J	J	Q	H	N	M
A	R	K	P	K	T	V	F	Y	P	O	E	C	C	W	U	M	Z	J	N
R	S	G	H	L	Y	L	G	L	O	L	V	K	Z	Y	D	M	F	C	B
D	M	U	R	P	H	Y	S	D	B	Z	Z	Y	R	S	D	W	Q	L	Q
N	X	G	W	P	S	G	P	E	F	Y	L	Z	Y	J	S	D	V	H	X
Z	T	J	H	Y	A	V	E	M	N	G	M	N	D	Z	G	X	M	K	B
J	J	F	L	X	U	F	Q	C	K	P	N	S	D	H	P	M	F	H	R
S	X	B	W	V	Q	W	R	L	S	V	B	M	G	B	Z	H	S	K	X
X	L	D	W	Y	S	M	B	Q	H	K	J	C	S	T	N	T	V	G	X

Author's last name (6)
David brought this for Marty to play with (4)
David's Aunt Pat is ___ to dogs (8)
David's hermit crab is his ___ (3)
David's last name (6)
Day on which SHILOH begins (6)
Food that gave Marty's schemes away (6)
Grocer's name (7)
Initials of Marty's home state (3)
Marty saw Judd shoot this animal (4)
Marty's age (6)
Marty's best friend's first name (5)
Marty's father said, 'You've got to go by the ___.' (3)
Marty's father's first name (3)
Marty's last name (7)
Marty's younger sister (5)
Name for David's hermit crab (6)
Name of Marty's new dog (6)
Owned the German Shepherd in the book (5)
Person who worked hard to earn Shiloh (5)

Shiloh was this kind of a dog (6)
Store having their catalogues delivered by mail (5)
The real owner of Shiloh (4)
Veterinarian's name: Doc ___ (6)
What David saw all over the dog pen (5)
What Grandma Preston is (6)
What Judd called some of his dogs (5)
What Judd signed about the dog (8)
What Marty and his father heard coming from the dog pen (5)
What Marty built for the dog (3)
What Marty called his mother (2)
What Marty threatened his sister Dara Lynn with (6)
What Marty told to keep Shiloh (4)

Shiloh Word Search 1 Answer Key

Words are placed backwards, forward, diagonally, up and down. Clues listed below can help you find the words. Circle the hidden vocabulary words in the maze.

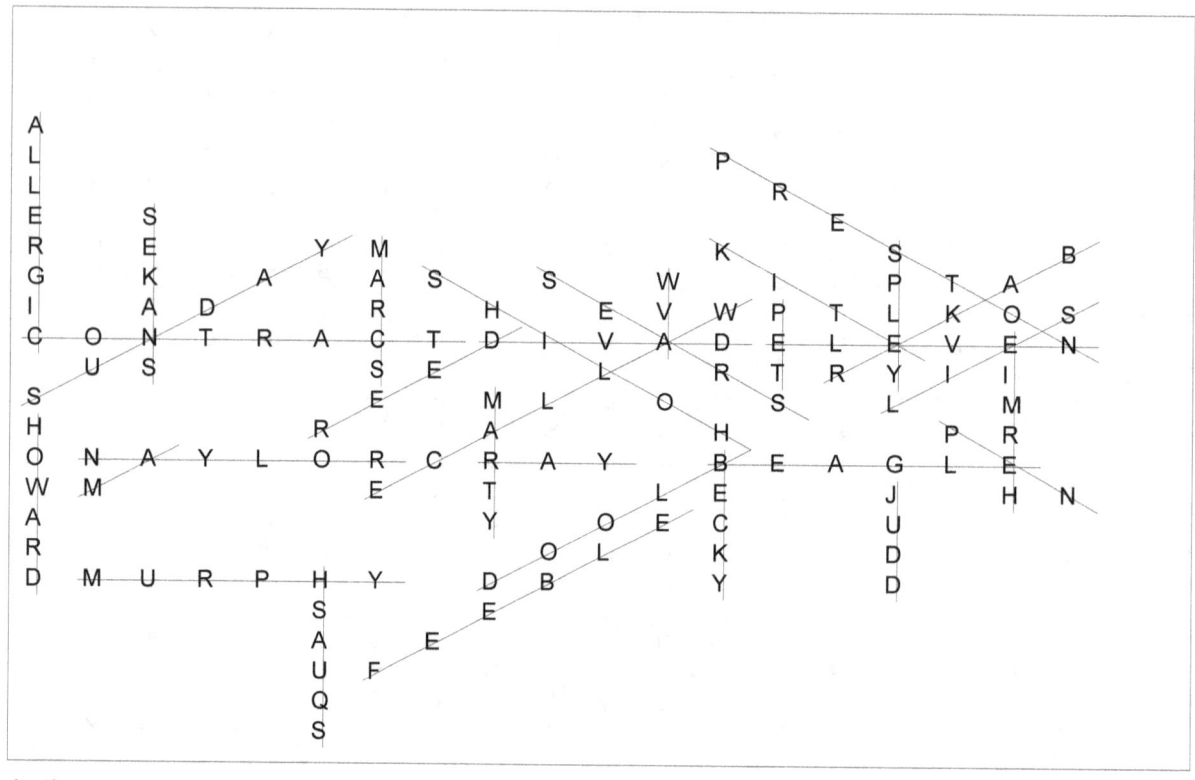

Author's last name (6)
David brought this for Marty to play with (4)
David's Aunt Pat is ___ to dogs (8)
David's hermit crab is his ___ (3)
David's last name (6)
Day on which SHILOH begins (6)
Food that gave Marty's schemes away (6)
Grocer's name (7)
Initials of Marty's home state (3)
Marty saw Judd shoot this animal (4)
Marty's age (6)
Marty's best friend's first name (5)
Marty's father said, 'You've got to go by the ___.' (3)
Marty's father's first name (3)
Marty's last name (7)
Marty's younger sister (5)
Name for David's hermit crab (6)
Name of Marty's new dog (6)
Owned the German Shepherd in the book (5)
Person who worked hard to earn Shiloh (5)

Shiloh was this kind of a dog (6)
Store having their catalogues delivered by mail (5)
The real owner of Shiloh (4)
Veterinarian's name: Doc ___ (6)
What David saw all over the dog pen (5)
What Grandma Preston is (6)
What Judd called some of his dogs (5)
What Judd signed about the dog (8)
What Marty and his father heard coming from the dog pen (5)
What Marty built for the dog (3)
What Marty called his mother (2)
What Marty threatened his sister Dara Lynn with (6)
What Marty told to keep Shiloh (4)

Shiloh Word Search 2

Words are placed backwards, forward, diagonally, up and down. Clues listed below can help you find the words. Circle the hidden vocabulary words in the maze.

```
Z Q D K P S Q C N M T W G R N V Z D H C
K H N B D H D T J Z P S K R S S N D W P
Y V K Q D T N K T W D Q S S R W H F Q W
R Q N G B J F S K F J G Z V L D J D Y Z
D T H B B X R E L W P F H C W B Q H M C
R Q G Y V Y M C Z F H E R M P B C P W G
A V D S S C Q A A J N E N H P E M C D N
W L H R D J Y L P L Z B W A C A V O D K
O G A Y X X M L E R L L R W Y G O Y M B
H E R M I E H A T D E E R W A L J U D D
S N G S U S Z W J B K Y R V B E O I Y D
R X M B A R S K W A W J W G K K V R V W
A L P U P X P R B B Y H S H I A H P J W
Y V Q M Q F L H V E X R N X D C J Z N N
D S Q A M Z E N Y C G E A K K Q B E F T
D M L R G W Y S D K P C K S S I V C Z T
S F B T Z P P W L Y C G E Q C E T T B P
S U D Y P R E S T O N O S B L R Y E V S
S Z N T N Z M Q T V R H N E K R A N W M
B S Y D P W H Y M G I G G T T X J M Q K
V K N P A W D G K L J W G P R Y C D N Z
K W S N H Y G N O L I E S B X A T R C M
L M J R D Z G H N K G V T V Y D C G F Z
N Y L J H Y G G X X J X C M Y V Z T P V
```

Author's last name (6)
David brought this for Marty to play with (4)
David's Aunt Pat is ___ to dogs (8)
David's hermit crab is his ___ (3)
David's last name (6)
Day on which SHILOH begins (6)
Food that gave Marty's schemes away (6)
Grocer's name (7)
Initials of Marty's home state (3)
Marty saw Judd shoot this animal (4)
Marty's age (6)
Marty's best friend's first name (5)
Marty's father said, 'You've got to go by the ___.' (3)
Marty's father's first name (3)
Marty's last name (7)
Marty's younger sister (5)
Name for David's hermit crab (6)
Name of Marty's new dog (6)
Owned the German Shepherd in the book (5)
Person who worked hard to earn Shiloh (5)
Shiloh was this kind of a dog (6)
Store having their catalogues delivered by mail (5)
The real owner of Shiloh (4)
Veterinarian's name: Doc ___ (6)
What David saw all over the dog pen (5)
What Grandma Preston is (6)
What Judd called some of his dogs (5)
What Judd signed about the dog (8)
What Marty and his father heard coming from the dog pen (5)
What Marty built for the dog (3)
What Marty called his mother (2)
What Marty threatened his sister Dara Lynn with (6)
What Marty told to keep Shiloh (4)

Shiloh Word Search 2 Answer Key

Words are placed backwards, forward, diagonally, up and down. Clues listed below can help you find the words. Circle the hidden vocabulary words in the maze.

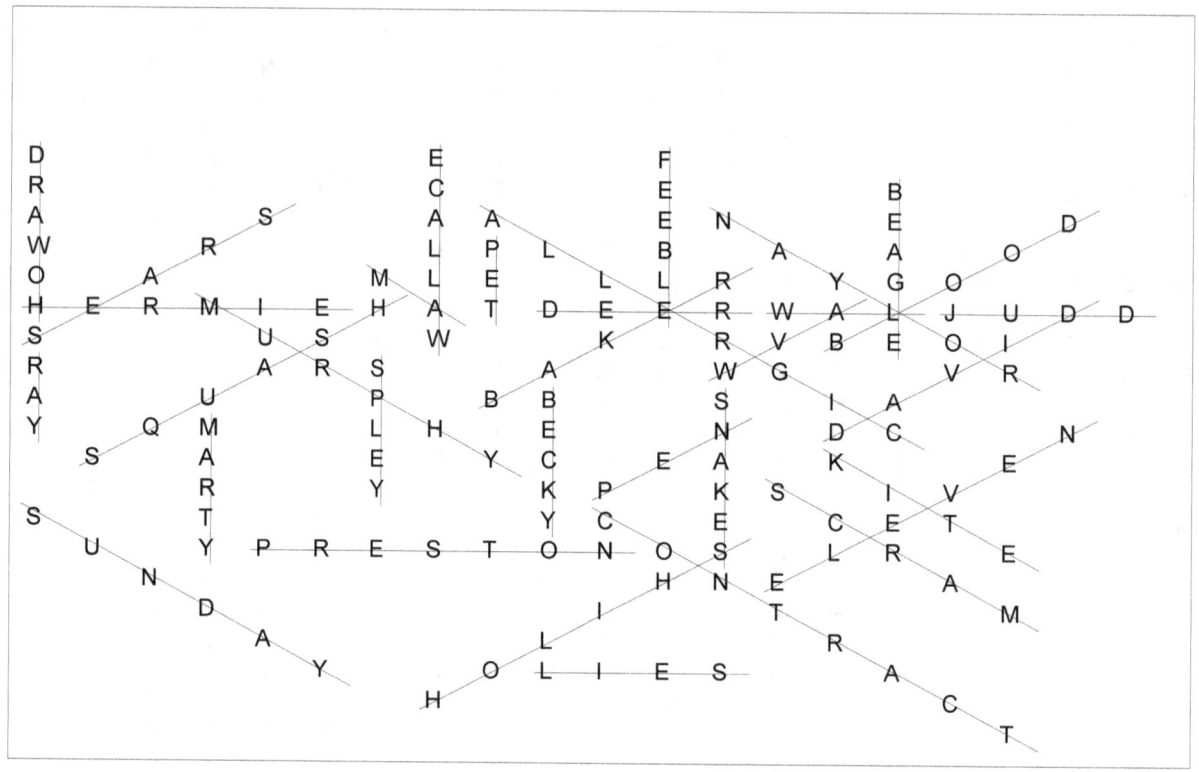

Author's last name (6)
David brought this for Marty to play with (4)
David's Aunt Pat is ___ to dogs (8)
David's hermit crab is his ___ (3)
David's last name (6)
Day on which SHILOH begins (6)
Food that gave Marty's schemes away (6)
Grocer's name (7)
Initials of Marty's home state (3)
Marty saw Judd shoot this animal (4)
Marty's age (6)
Marty's best friend's first name (5)
Marty's father said, 'You've got to go by the ___.' (3)
Marty's father's first name (3)
Marty's last name (7)
Marty's younger sister (5)
Name for David's hermit crab (6)
Name of Marty's new dog (6)
Owned the German Shepherd in the book (5)
Person who worked hard to earn Shiloh (5)

Shiloh was this kind of a dog (6)
Store having their catalogues delivered by mail (5)
The real owner of Shiloh (4)
Veterinarian's name: Doc ___ (6)
What David saw all over the dog pen (5)
What Grandma Preston is (6)
What Judd called some of his dogs (5)
What Judd signed about the dog (8)
What Marty and his father heard coming from the dog pen (5)
What Marty built for the dog (3)
What Marty called his mother (2)
What Marty threatened his sister Dara Lynn with (6)
What Marty told to keep Shiloh (4)

Shiloh Word Search 3

Words are placed backwards, forward, diagonally, up and down. Words listed below are included in the maze. Circle the hidden vocabulary words in the maze.

```
T Z D V D Z C Q V J N K C L M X S K C H
B X J H Q X B X P R P M P J R X X T P Y
W T W L L Z H G G X X P W A W R B B M K
F T J K T E X Y F S S K T V R V S N L C
T Z T C L S M J K R V W W W A L L A C E
Y K F G A L U M G O F Z M G D V M F L B
G G A D L T G N W L K K U P K H F B G W
M E K H L S R X D Y Y V R F R H E W G R
B B A K E R S Q U A S H P E N E V E L E
Q V S A R R Z F R N Y N H E F D S N L C
V Z R D G J M H L X L V Y S T Z B T H G
X S C V I S Z I I N Y Y E P G C D G O W
D P M P C D P Y E T I K B L O O D M L N
E G R A R T Z E S F A N J P J N W Y I R
E N D A R P L L S N D T V Z L T Q G H P
R T W D J T H P S J A L A W F R X X S M
Y O D J K X Y S Z Z V X X Z M A P B B D
H U T Z D T J Y R V I G X V T C H F G Q
J D W X X H L R Y Z D X V B D T G F D T
H S G R P S L L W C C V G R P X N Y V H
P D C K Y R Q Y R G W V Z P W Z V T Y P
H Q H R S T Q F Q T M F L Q D G G T M R
D J S V A C G M K P V D Y V N S Y L X F
P Z R P Y M P P Y T F G T B S Y X F Q X
```

ALLERGIC	DEER	LAW	PET	SQUASH
BAKER	ELEVEN	LIES	PRESTON	SUNDAY
BEAGLE	FEEBLE	MA	RAY	WALLACE
BECKY	HERMIE	MARTY	SCRAM	WVA
BLOOD	HOWARD	MURPHY	SEARS	YELPS
CONTRACT	JUDD	NAYLOR	SHILOH	
DAVID	KITE	PEN	SNAKES	

Shiloh Word Search 3 Answer Key

Words are placed backwards, forward, diagonally, up and down. Words listed below are included in the maze. Circle the hidden vocabulary words in the maze.

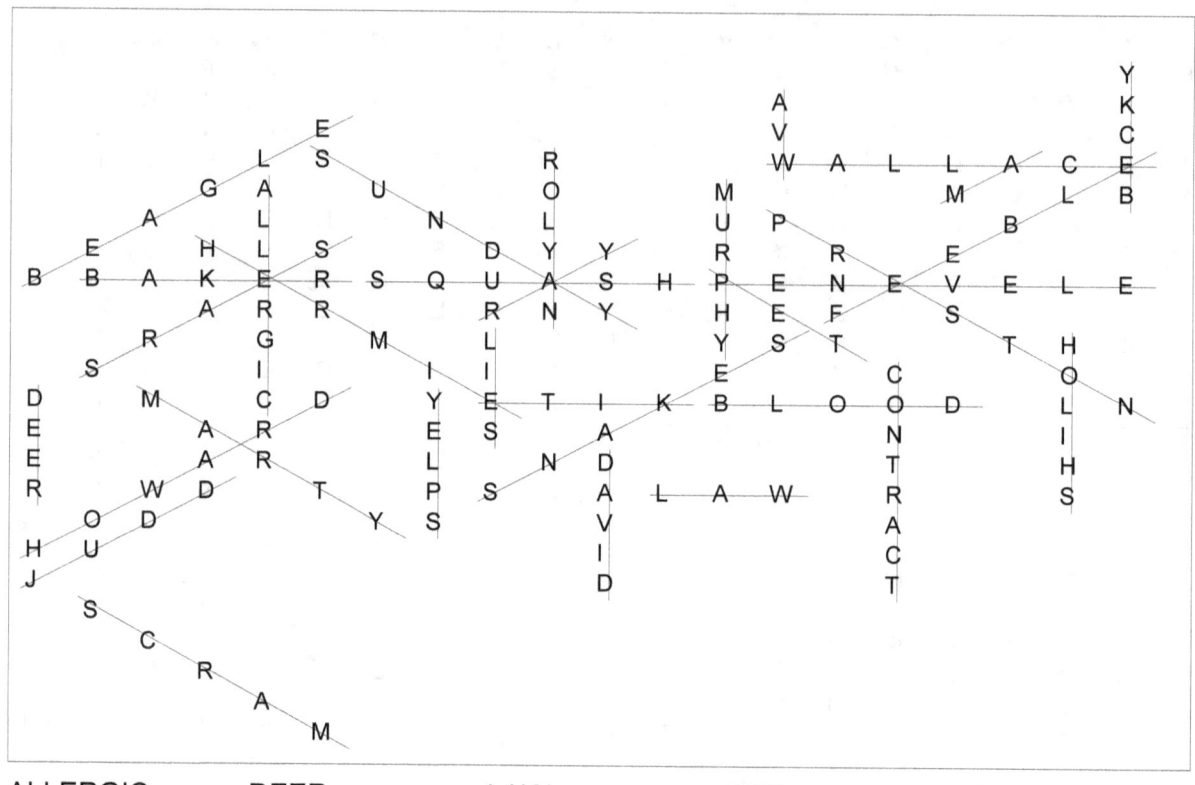

ALLERGIC	DEER	LAW	PET	SQUASH
BAKER	ELEVEN	LIES	PRESTON	SUNDAY
BEAGLE	FEEBLE	MA	RAY	WALLACE
BECKY	HERMIE	MARTY	SCRAM	WVA
BLOOD	HOWARD	MURPHY	SEARS	YELPS
CONTRACT	JUDD	NAYLOR	SHILOH	
DAVID	KITE	PEN	SNAKES	

Shiloh Word Search 4

Words are placed backwards, forward, diagonally, up and down. Words listed below are included in the maze. Circle the hidden vocabulary words in the maze.

S	E	A	R	S	M	S	H	H	B	E	C	K	Y	E	V	D	S	P	K
E	U	F	N	R	A	P	N	G	Z	L	B	K	L	D	I	R	C	R	R
I	E	N	E	N	R	L	A	A	Y	B	V	G	P	V	J	A	R	E	S
L	C	K	D	X	T	E	L	G	K	E	A	F	A	C	L	W	A	S	V
P	A	O	T	A	Y	Y	L	T	X	E	M	D	Z	N	L	O	M	T	C
B	L	T	N	P	Y	Y	E	C	B	F	S	N	W	F	A	H	X	O	K
K	L	W	C	T	S	Z	R	Z	B	B	G	A	P	W	J	Y	V	N	M
Y	A	M	V	Q	R	H	G	H	N	S	V	H	B	L	B	Z	L	Y	W
K	W	H	T	G	F	A	I	D	V	W	X	V	C	G	Z	B	X	O	Y
D	Z	R	F	F	Q	F	C	L	F	N	V	Z	L	M	Z	T	K	Z	R
N	S	T	R	N	B	Q	Z	T	O	D	H	D	J	L	X	M	N	P	M
B	D	N	P	R	J	W	Q	F	P	H	L	R	S	J	L	K	T	H	Y
K	P	T	J	D	R	Z	B	H	S	B	J	V	F	X	R	R	K	T	D
H	D	W	H	W	N	P	N	M	B	V	Q	J	H	V	H	X	X	Z	P
C	V	Y	S	W	Y	S	R	L	M	Q	K	X	F	P	Q	T	C	G	Z
M	N	J	G	W	W	X	Z	N	F	H	X	W	X	L	F	T	M	F	X
M	N	H	P	W	N	Z	N	J	X	N	W	Y	X	Q	D	X	S	G	Y
L	C	X	W	J	D	J	X	Y	M	Q	D	P	N	D	D	J	N	J	F
W	H	G	M	B	N	N	N	V	H	G	J	B	C	X	W	G	W	L	V
N	E	H	W	X	E	K	Q	S	V	C	X	Z	R	Y	T	Y	W	Y	J
T	R	G	C	V	M	S	A	J	Y	X	F	G	Y	Q	R	L	R	D	R
X	M	B	E	Q	Z	U	J	L	U	P	L	Z	N	S	W	F	A	G	B
Z	I	L	W	V	Q	A	M	Z	X	D	E	M	U	R	P	H	Y	W	Q
D	E	E	R	S	M	B	L	O	O	D	D	T	K	I	T	E	P	E	N

ALLERGIC	DEER	LAW	PET	SQUASH
BAKER	ELEVEN	LIES	PRESTON	SUNDAY
BEAGLE	FEEBLE	MA	RAY	WALLACE
BECKY	HERMIE	MARTY	SCRAM	WVA
BLOOD	HOWARD	MURPHY	SEARS	YELPS
CONTRACT	JUDD	NAYLOR	SHILOH	
DAVID	KITE	PEN	SNAKES	

Shiloh Word Search 4 Answer Key

Words are placed backwards, forward, diagonally, up and down. Words listed below are included in the maze. Circle the hidden vocabulary words in the maze.

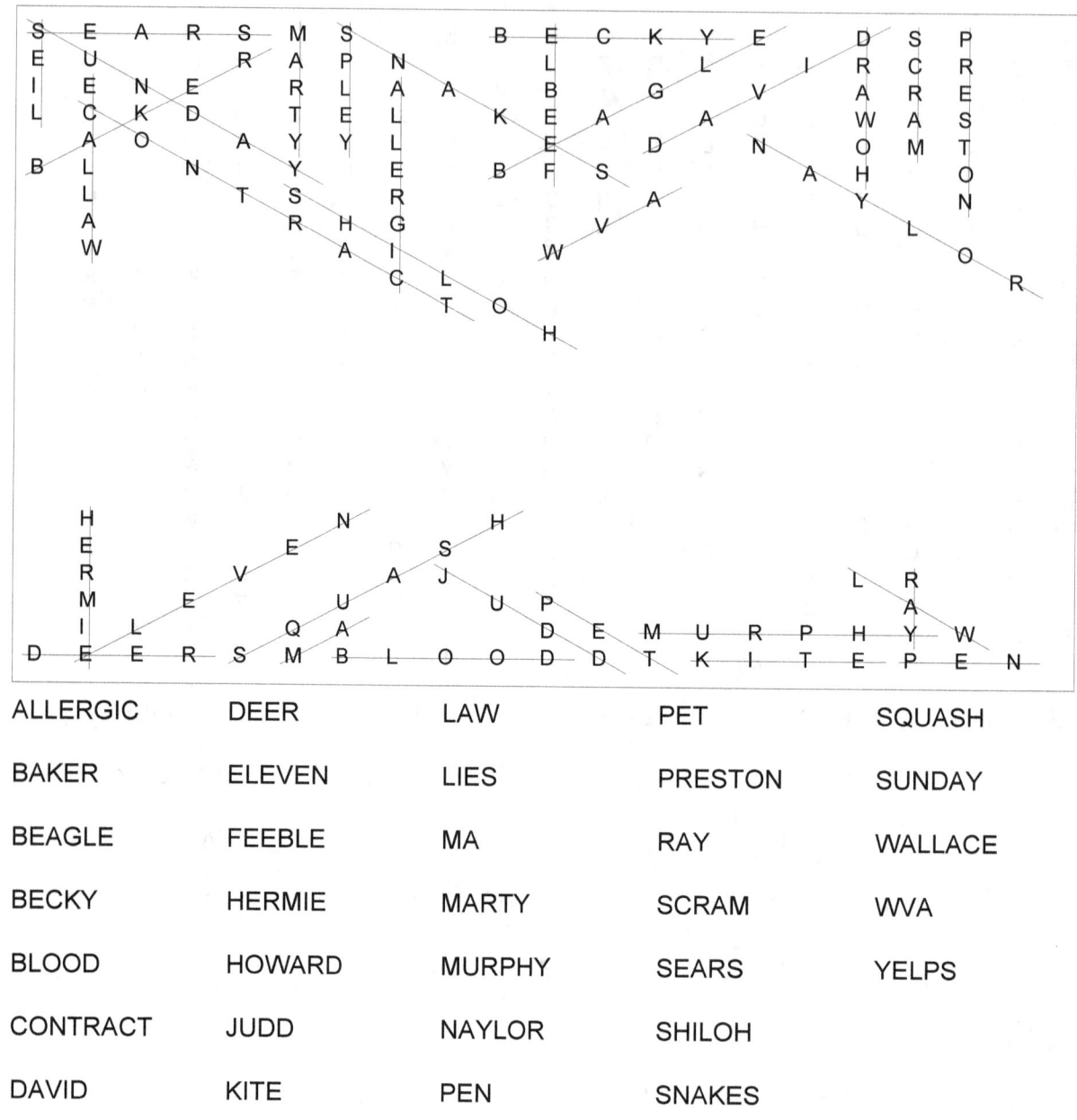

ALLERGIC	DEER	LAW	PET	SQUASH
BAKER	ELEVEN	LIES	PRESTON	SUNDAY
BEAGLE	FEEBLE	MA	RAY	WALLACE
BECKY	HERMIE	MARTY	SCRAM	WVA
BLOOD	HOWARD	MURPHY	SEARS	YELPS
CONTRACT	JUDD	NAYLOR	SHILOH	
DAVID	KITE	PEN	SNAKES	

Shiloh Crossword 1

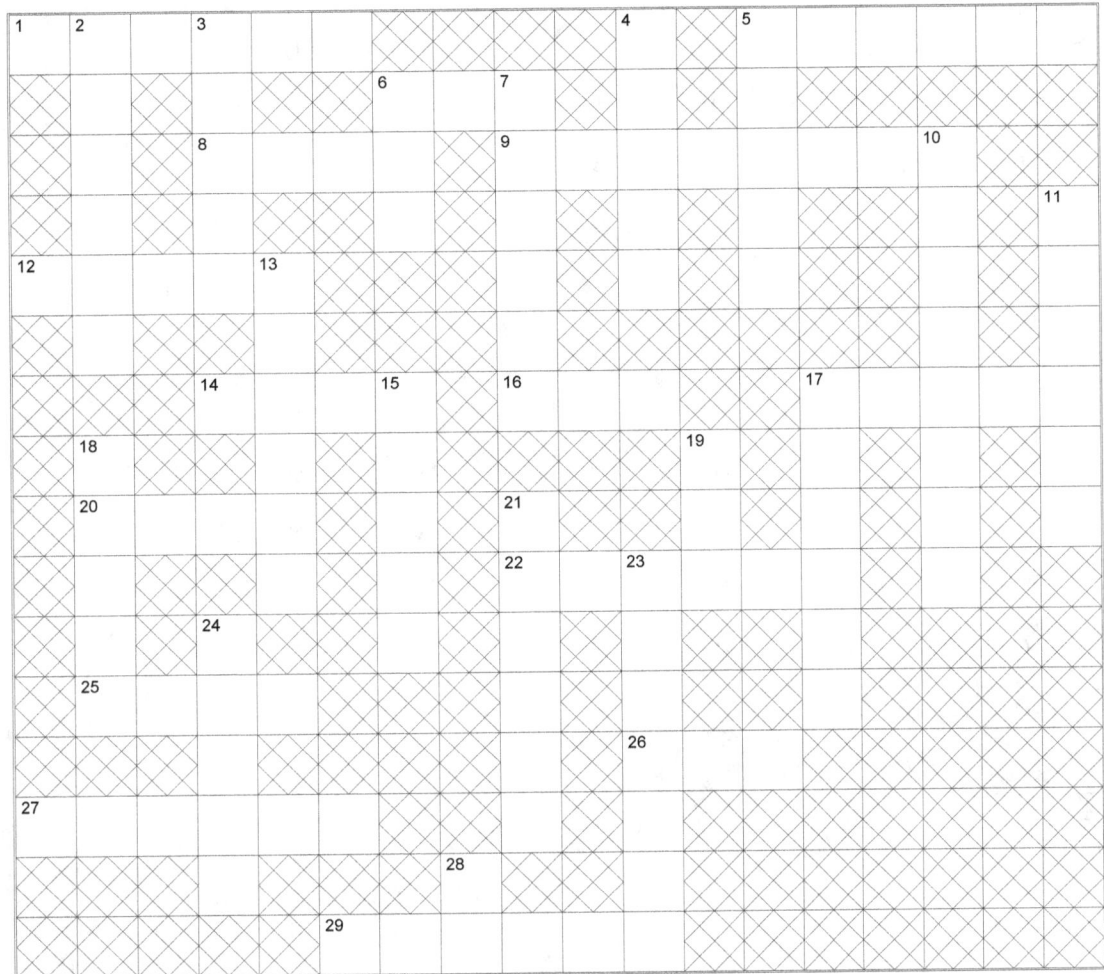

Across
1. What Grandma Preston is
5. Veterinarian's name: Doc ___
6. What Marty built for the dog
8. David brought this for Marty to play with
9. David's Aunt Pat is ___ to dogs
12. Store having their catalogues delivered by mail
14. The real owner of Shiloh
16. Marty's father's first name
17. What Judd called some of his dogs
20. What Marty told to keep Shiloh
22. David's last name
25. Marty saw Judd shoot this animal
26. Marty's father said, 'You've got to go by the ___.'
27. What Marty threatened his sister Dara Lynn with
29. Shiloh was this kind of a dog

Down
2. Marty's age
3. Owned the German Shepherd in the book
4. What Marty and his father heard coming from the dog pen
5. Person who worked hard to earn Shiloh
6. David's hermit crab is his ___
7. Author's last name
10. What Judd signed about the dog
11. Name for David's hermit crab
13. Food that gave Marty's schemes away
15. Marty's best friend's first name
17. Day on which SHILOH begins
18. What David saw all over the dog pen
19. Initials of Marty's home state
21. Name of Marty's new dog
23. Grocer's name
24. Marty's younger sister
28. What Marty called his mother

Shiloh Crossword 1 Answer Key

	1 F	2 E	3 B	L	E				4 Y		5 M	U	R	P	H	Y
		L	A				6 P	7 N		E		A				
		E	8 K	I	T	E		9 A	L	L	E	R	G	I	10 C	
		V	E			T		Y		P		T			O	11 H
	12 S	E	A	13 R	S			L		S		Y			N	E
		N		Q				O							T	R
			14 J	U	D	15 D		16 R	A	Y			17 S	C	R	A	M
	18 B		A			A					19 W		U		A	I
	20 L	I	E	S		V		21 S			V		N		C	E
	O			H		I		22 H	O	23 W	A	R	D		T	
	O		24 B			D		I		A			A			
	25 D	E	E	R				L		L			Y			
			C					O		26 L	A	W				
	27 S	N	A	K	E	S		H		A						
			Y			28 M		A		C						
					29 B	E	A	G	L	E						

Across
1. What Grandma Preston is
5. Veterinarian's name: Doc ___
6. What Marty built for the dog
8. David brought this for Marty to play with
9. David's Aunt Pat is ___ to dogs
12. Store having their catalogues delivered by mail
14. The real owner of Shiloh
16. Marty's father's first name
17. What Judd called some of his dogs
20. What Marty told to keep Shiloh
22. David's last name
25. Marty saw Judd shoot this animal
26. Marty's father said, 'You've got to go by the ___.'
27. What Marty threatened his sister Dara Lynn with
29. Shiloh was this kind of a dog

Down
2. Marty's age
3. Owned the German Shepherd in the book
4. What Marty and his father heard coming from the dog pen
5. Person who worked hard to earn Shiloh
6. David's hermit crab is his ___
7. Author's last name
10. What Judd signed about the dog
11. Name for David's hermit crab
13. Food that gave Marty's schemes away
15. Marty's best friend's first name
17. Day on which SHILOH begins
18. What David saw all over the dog pen
19. Initials of Marty's home state
21. Name of Marty's new dog
23. Grocer's name
24. Marty's younger sister
28. What Marty called his mother

Shiloh Crossword 2

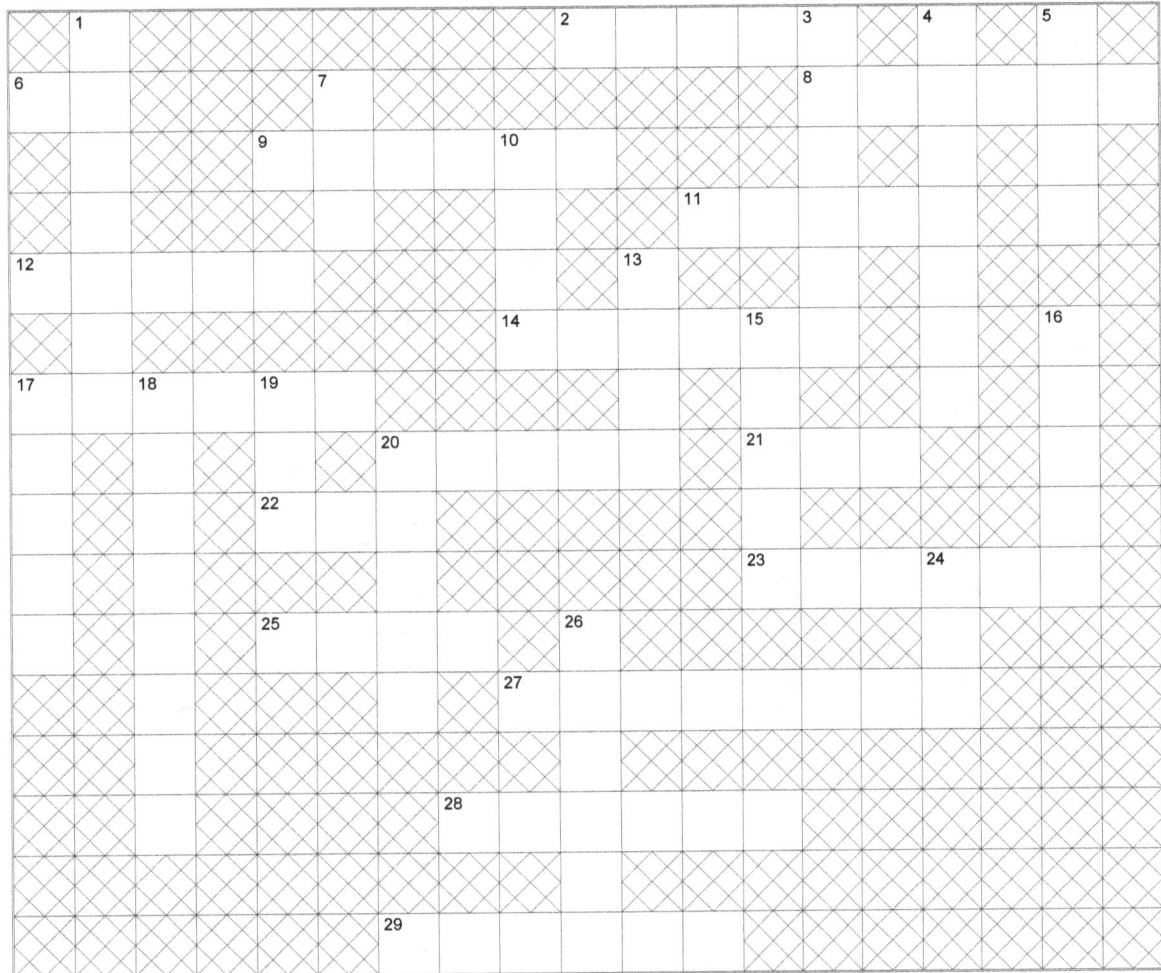

Across
2. Store having their catalogues delivered by mail
6. What Marty called his mother
8. Name for David's hermit crab
9. What Grandma Preston is
11. What Marty and his father heard coming from the dog pen
12. Marty's best friend's first name
14. Food that gave Marty's schemes away
17. Shiloh was this kind of a dog
20. What David saw all over the dog pen
21. Marty's father's first name
22. Initials of Marty's home state
23. Veterinarian's name: Doc ___
25. Marty saw Judd shoot this animal
27. What Judd signed about the dog
28. What Marty threatened his sister Dara Lynn with
29. Day on which SHILOH begins

Down
1. Grocer's name
3. Name of Marty's new dog
4. Marty's last name
5. David brought this for Marty to play with
7. What Marty built for the dog
10. What Marty told to keep Shiloh
13. The real owner of Shiloh
15. What Judd called some of his dogs
16. Person who worked hard to earn Shiloh
17. Marty's younger sister
18. David's Aunt Pat is ___ to dogs
19. Marty's father said, 'You've got to go by the ___.'
20. Owned the German Shepherd in the book
24. David's hermit crab is his ___
26. David's last name

Shiloh Crossword 2 Answer Key

		1 W			2 S	E	A	3 R	S		4 P		5 K	
6 M	A			7 P				8 H	E	R	M	I	E	
	L		9 F	E	E	10 B	L	E			E		T	
	L		N			I		11 Y	E	L	P	S	E	
12 D	A	V	I	D		E		13 J		O	T			
	C				14 S	Q	U	A	15 S	H		16 M		
17 B	18 E	19 A	G	L	E			D	C			N	A	
E	L	A		20 B	L	O	O	D	21 R	A	Y		R	
C	L	22 W	V	A					A				T	
K	E			K				23 M	U	R	24 P	H	Y	
Y	R	25 D	E	E	R		26 H				E			
	G			R		27 C	O	N	T	R	A	C	T	
	I						W							
	C			28 S	N	A	K	E	S					
							R							
				29 S	U	N	D	A	Y					

Across
2. Store having their catalogues delivered by mail
6. What Marty called his mother
8. Name for David's hermit crab
9. What Grandma Preston is
11. What Marty and his father heard coming from the dog pen
12. Marty's best friend's first name
14. Food that gave Marty's schemes away
17. Shiloh was this kind of a dog
20. What David saw all over the dog pen
21. Marty's father's first name
22. Initials of Marty's home state
23. Veterinarian's name: Doc ___
25. Marty saw Judd shoot this animal
27. What Judd signed about the dog
28. What Marty threatened his sister Dara Lynn with
29. Day on which SHILOH begins

Down
1. Grocer's name
3. Name of Marty's new dog
4. Marty's last name
5. David brought this for Marty to play with
7. What Marty built for the dog
10. What Marty told to keep Shiloh
13. The real owner of Shiloh
15. What Judd called some of his dogs
16. Person who worked hard to earn Shiloh
17. Marty's younger sister
18. David's Aunt Pat is ___ to dogs
19. Marty's father said, 'You've got to go by the ___.'
20. Owned the German Shepherd in the book
24. David's hermit crab is his ___
26. David's last name

Shiloh Crossword 3

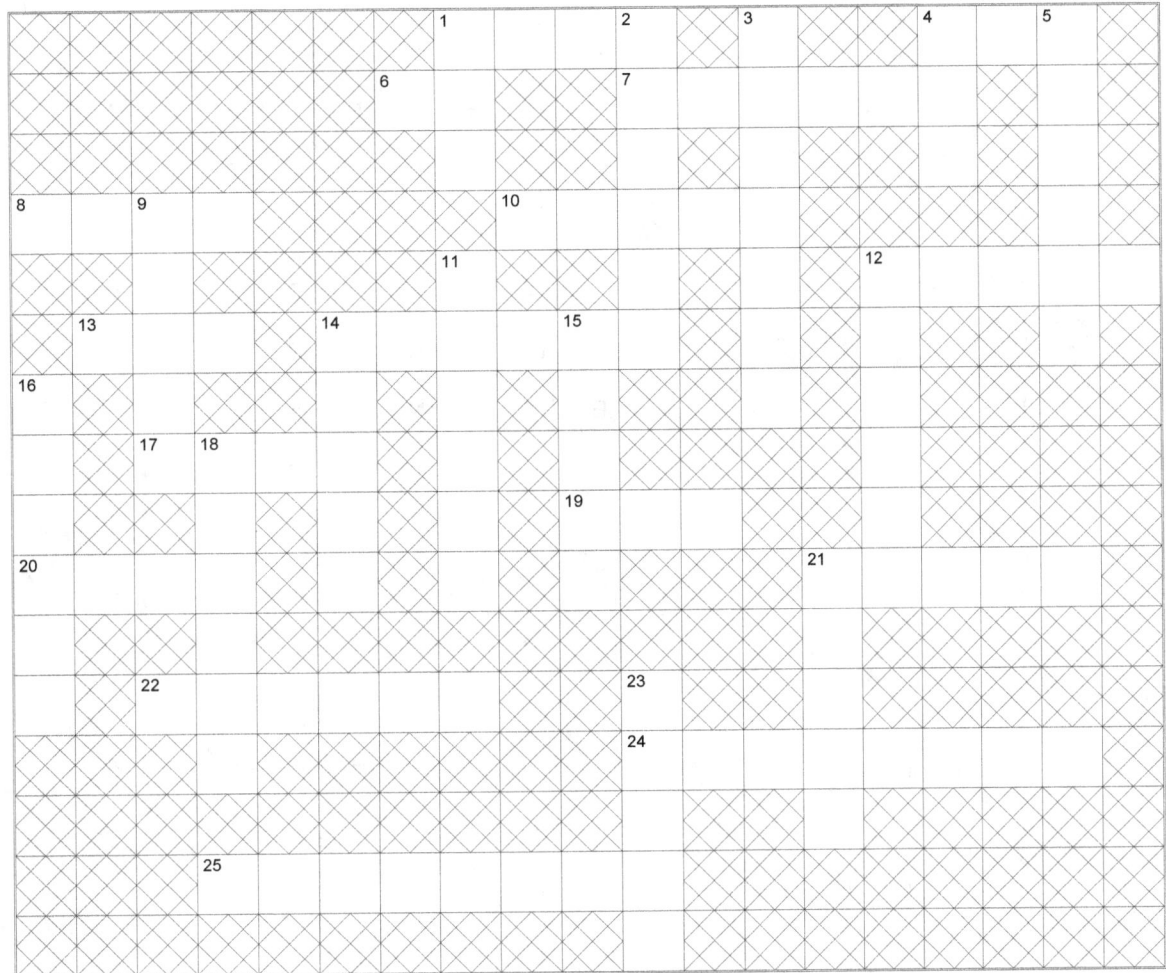

Across
1. What Marty told to keep Shiloh
4. What Marty built for the dog
6. What Marty called his mother
7. Name for David's hermit crab
8. The real owner of Shiloh
10. What Marty and his father heard coming from the dog pen
12. What David saw all over the dog pen
13. Initials of Marty's home state
14. Food that gave Marty's schemes away
17. Marty saw Judd shoot this animal
19. Marty's father's first name
20. David brought this for Marty to play with
21. Marty's younger sister
22. What Grandma Preston is
24. David's Aunt Pat is ___ to dogs
25. What Judd signed about the dog

Down
1. Marty's father said, 'You've got to go by the ___.'
2. Name of Marty's new dog
3. Marty's last name
4. David's hermit crab is his ___
5. Author's last name
9. Marty's best friend's first name
11. Day on which SHILOH begins
12. Shiloh was this kind of a dog
14. What Judd called some of his dogs
15. Store having their catalogues delivered by mail
16. What Marty threatened his sister Dara Lynn with
18. Marty's age
21. Owned the German Shepherd in the book
23. Person who worked hard to earn Shiloh

Shiloh Crossword 3 Answer Key

								¹L	I	E	²S		³P			⁴P	E	⁵N
						⁶M	A				⁷H	E	R	M	I	E		A
						W					I		E			T		Y
⁸J	U	⁹D	D					¹⁰Y	E	L	P	S						L
		A					¹¹S				O		T		¹²B	L	O	O	D
		¹³W	V	A	¹⁴S	Q	U	A	¹⁵S	H		O		E			R
¹⁶S		I			C		N		E			N		A			
N		¹⁷D	¹⁸E	E	R		D		A					G			
A			L		A		A		¹⁹R	A	Y			L			
²⁰K	I	T	E		M		Y		S				²¹B	E	C	K	Y
E			V										A				
S		²²F	E	E	B	L	E			²³M			K				
			N						²⁴A	L	L	E	R	G	I	C	
										R			R				
			²⁵C	O	N	T	R	A	C	T							
										Y							

Across
1. What Marty told to keep Shiloh
4. What Marty built for the dog
6. What Marty called his mother
7. Name for David's hermit crab
8. The real owner of Shiloh
10. What Marty and his father heard coming from the dog pen
12. What David saw all over the dog pen
13. Initials of Marty's home state
14. Food that gave Marty's schemes away
17. Marty saw Judd shoot this animal
19. Marty's father's first name
20. David brought this for Marty to play with
21. Marty's younger sister
22. What Grandma Preston is
24. David's Aunt Pat is ___ to dogs
25. What Judd signed about the dog

Down
1. Marty's father said, 'You've got to go by the ___.'
2. Name of Marty's new dog
3. Marty's last name
4. David's hermit crab is his ___
5. Author's last name
9. Marty's best friend's first name
11. Day on which SHILOH begins
12. Shiloh was this kind of a dog
14. What Judd called some of his dogs
15. Store having their catalogues delivered by mail
16. What Marty threatened his sister Dara Lynn with
18. Marty's age
21. Owned the German Shepherd in the book
23. Person who worked hard to earn Shiloh

Shiloh Crossword 4

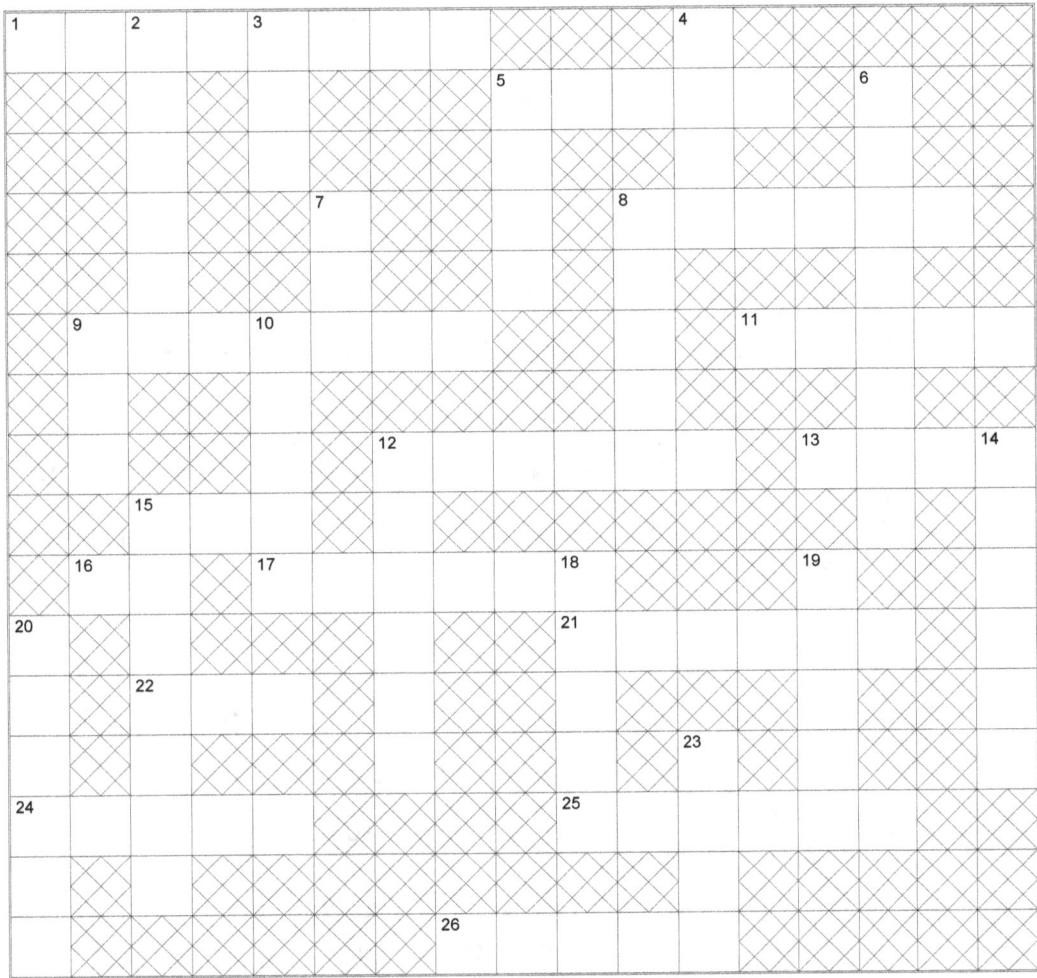

Across
1. What Judd signed about the dog
5. Marty's best friend's first name
8. Shiloh was this kind of a dog
9. Marty's last name
11. Person who worked hard to earn Shiloh
12. David's last name
13. What Marty told to keep Shiloh
15. Initials of Marty's home state
16. What Marty called his mother
17. Veterinarian's name: Doc ___
21. Marty's age
22. Marty's father said, 'You've got to go by the ___.'
24. Marty's younger sister
25. Food that gave Marty's schemes away
26. What David saw all over the dog pen

Down
2. Author's last name
3. Marty's father's first name
4. David brought this for Marty to play with
5. Marty saw Judd shoot this animal
6. David's Aunt Pat is ___ to dogs
7. David's hermit crab is his ___
8. Owned the German Shepherd in the book
9. What Marty built for the dog
10. What Judd called some of his dogs
12. Name for David's hermit crab
14. Name of Marty's new dog
15. Grocer's name
18. What Marty and his father heard coming from the dog pen
19. Store having their catalogues delivered by mail
20. What Grandma Preston is
23. The real owner of Shiloh

Shiloh Crossword 4 Answer Key

	1 C	2 O	N	3 T	R	A	C	T			4 K			
		A		A			5 D	A	V	I	D		6 A	
		Y		Y			E				T		L	
		L			7 P		E		8 B	E	A	G	L	E
		O			E		R		A				E	
	9 P	R	E	10 S	T	O	N		K		11 M	A	R	T Y
	E			C					E		G			
	N			R		12 H	O	W	A	R	D	13 L	I	E 14 S
		15 W	V	A		E						C		H
	16 M	A		17 M	U	R	P	H	18 Y		19 S			I
20 F		L			M				21 E	L	E	V	E	N L
		22 L	A	W		I			L				A	O
E		A				E			P		23 J		R	H
24 B	E	C	K	Y					25 S	Q	U	A	S	H
L			E								D			
E						26 B	L	O	O	D				

Across
1. What Judd signed about the dog
5. Marty's best friend's first name
8. Shiloh was this kind of a dog
9. Marty's last name
11. Person who worked hard to earn Shiloh
12. David's last name
13. What Marty told to keep Shiloh
15. Initials of Marty's home state
16. What Marty called his mother
17. Veterinarian's name: Doc ___
21. Marty's age
22. Marty's father said, 'You've got to go by the ___.'
24. Marty's younger sister
25. Food that gave Marty's schemes away
26. What David saw all over the dog pen

Down
2. Author's last name
3. Marty's father's first name
4. David brought this for Marty to play with
5. Marty saw Judd shoot this animal
6. David's Aunt Pat is ___ to dogs
7. David's hermit crab is his ___
8. Owned the German Shepherd in the book
9. What Marty built for the dog
10. What Judd called some of his dogs
12. Name for David's hermit crab
14. Name of Marty's new dog
15. Grocer's name
18. What Marty and his father heard coming from the dog pen
19. Store having their catalogues delivered by mail
20. What Grandma Preston is
23. The real owner of Shiloh

Shiloh

MA	PEN	JUDD	LIES	HOWARD
ALLERGIC	SHILOH	PRESTON	PET	SUNDAY
ELEVEN	NAYLOR	FREE SPACE	WVA	MARTY
CONTRACT	RAY	BLOOD	FEEBLE	SQUASH
SEARS	BECKY	LAW	DAVID	DEER

Shiloh

MURPHY	SCRAM	KITE	SNAKES	BAKER
HERMIE	WALLACE	YELPS	DEER	DAVID
LAW	BECKY	FREE SPACE	SQUASH	FEEBLE
BLOOD	RAY	CONTRACT	MARTY	WVA
BEAGLE	NAYLOR	ELEVEN	SUNDAY	PET

Shiloh

HOWARD	BLOOD	MURPHY	SUNDAY	WVA
KITE	DAVID	MA	DEER	BECKY
YELPS	WALLACE	FREE SPACE	PET	SHILOH
CONTRACT	ELEVEN	PRESTON	HERMIE	LAW
BAKER	RAY	BEAGLE	FEEBLE	SNAKES

Shiloh

SCRAM	MARTY	JUDD	NAYLOR	SQUASH
LIES	SEARS	PEN	SNAKES	FEEBLE
BEAGLE	RAY	FREE SPACE	LAW	HERMIE
PRESTON	ELEVEN	CONTRACT	SHILOH	PET
ALLERGIC	WALLACE	YELPS	BECKY	DEER

Shiloh

HOWARD	BEAGLE	BLOOD	SNAKES	BECKY
SCRAM	YELPS	KITE	WALLACE	ALLERGIC
JUDD	MURPHY	FREE SPACE	SHILOH	CONTRACT
DAVID	PET	BAKER	RAY	MA
SUNDAY	HERMIE	WVA	ELEVEN	DEER

Shiloh

SEARS	MARTY	SQUASH	FEEBLE	LAW
PEN	NAYLOR	LIES	DEER	ELEVEN
WVA	HERMIE	FREE SPACE	MA	RAY
BAKER	PET	DAVID	CONTRACT	SHILOH
PRESTON	MURPHY	JUDD	ALLERGIC	WALLACE

Shiloh

SCRAM	SUNDAY	MARTY	HOWARD	WALLACE
BLOOD	CONTRACT	BEAGLE	BECKY	FEEBLE
PEN	SQUASH	FREE SPACE	PRESTON	JUDD
PET	MURPHY	BAKER	LAW	SNAKES
KITE	DEER	SHILOH	SEARS	HERMIE

Shiloh

NAYLOR	ALLERGIC	YELPS	ELEVEN	WVA
DAVID	LIES	MA	HERMIE	SEARS
SHILOH	DEER	FREE SPACE	SNAKES	LAW
BAKER	MURPHY	PET	JUDD	PRESTON
RAY	SQUASH	PEN	FEEBLE	BECKY

Shiloh

MARTY	PRESTON	WVA	LAW	SCRAM
ALLERGIC	MA	BECKY	KITE	SEARS
ELEVEN	MURPHY	FREE SPACE	NAYLOR	LIES
JUDD	HOWARD	PEN	BLOOD	DAVID
RAY	YELPS	SHILOH	CONTRACT	BEAGLE

Shiloh

BAKER	WALLACE	PET	SUNDAY	DEER
HERMIE	SNAKES	FEEBLE	BEAGLE	CONTRACT
SHILOH	YELPS	FREE SPACE	DAVID	BLOOD
PEN	HOWARD	JUDD	LIES	NAYLOR
SQUASH	MURPHY	ELEVEN	SEARS	KITE

Shiloh

SQUASH	BECKY	PEN	MARTY	ALLERGIC
NAYLOR	BEAGLE	LAW	SUNDAY	WVA
LIES	MURPHY	FREE SPACE	HOWARD	PRESTON
PET	SHILOH	DEER	CONTRACT	KITE
MA	ELEVEN	BLOOD	FEEBLE	SEARS

Shiloh

BAKER	HERMIE	DAVID	YELPS	RAY
WALLACE	SNAKES	JUDD	SEARS	FEEBLE
BLOOD	ELEVEN	FREE SPACE	KITE	CONTRACT
DEER	SHILOH	PET	PRESTON	HOWARD
SCRAM	MURPHY	LIES	WVA	SUNDAY

Shiloh

LIES	BLOOD	SQUASH	WVA	CONTRACT
MARTY	SUNDAY	MURPHY	PRESTON	ELEVEN
HOWARD	RAY	FREE SPACE	HERMIE	JUDD
MA	DEER	FEEBLE	WALLACE	SNAKES
PET	ALLERGIC	PEN	SEARS	BEAGLE

Shiloh

SCRAM	LAW	BAKER	YELPS	KITE
BECKY	SHILOH	DAVID	BEAGLE	SEARS
PEN	ALLERGIC	FREE SPACE	SNAKES	WALLACE
FEEBLE	DEER	MA	JUDD	HERMIE
NAYLOR	RAY	HOWARD	ELEVEN	PRESTON

Shiloh

FEEBLE	BEAGLE	PRESTON	SNAKES	ELEVEN
MA	SHILOH	JUDD	MURPHY	NAYLOR
SQUASH	BLOOD	FREE SPACE	BAKER	ALLERGIC
KITE	DEER	SEARS	WVA	PET
WALLACE	CONTRACT	SCRAM	BECKY	RAY

Shiloh

LIES	HERMIE	LAW	PEN	YELPS
SUNDAY	DAVID	MARTY	RAY	BECKY
SCRAM	CONTRACT	FREE SPACE	PET	WVA
SEARS	DEER	KITE	ALLERGIC	BAKER
HOWARD	BLOOD	SQUASH	NAYLOR	MURPHY

Shiloh

BEAGLE	SEARS	DAVID	MA	DEER
BAKER	SNAKES	ALLERGIC	LAW	PET
MURPHY	ELEVEN	FREE SPACE	SCRAM	MARTY
PEN	CONTRACT	JUDD	BECKY	HOWARD
SUNDAY	SQUASH	BLOOD	KITE	NAYLOR

Shiloh

RAY	WVA	SHILOH	FEEBLE	WALLACE
YELPS	HERMIE	PRESTON	NAYLOR	KITE
BLOOD	SQUASH	FREE SPACE	HOWARD	BECKY
JUDD	CONTRACT	PEN	MARTY	SCRAM
LIES	ELEVEN	MURPHY	PET	LAW

Shiloh

PRESTON	JUDD	FEEBLE	BLOOD	SUNDAY
HOWARD	SNAKES	RAY	MURPHY	DEER
LIES	YELPS	FREE SPACE	SCRAM	WALLACE
SEARS	KITE	ELEVEN	BEAGLE	BECKY
BAKER	PET	CONTRACT	HERMIE	DAVID

Shiloh

SQUASH	MARTY	WVA	SHILOH	MA
NAYLOR	PEN	LAW	DAVID	HERMIE
CONTRACT	PET	FREE SPACE	BECKY	BEAGLE
ELEVEN	KITE	SEARS	WALLACE	SCRAM
ALLERGIC	YELPS	LIES	DEER	MURPHY

Shiloh

SNAKES	PRESTON	MA	PET	DEER
SCRAM	HERMIE	SUNDAY	RAY	BAKER
KITE	MARTY	FREE SPACE	MURPHY	SHILOH
BLOOD	YELPS	ELEVEN	CONTRACT	JUDD
LIES	DAVID	HOWARD	LAW	BECKY

Shiloh

BEAGLE	WVA	NAYLOR	PEN	FEEBLE
ALLERGIC	WALLACE	SQUASH	BECKY	LAW
HOWARD	DAVID	FREE SPACE	JUDD	CONTRACT
ELEVEN	YELPS	BLOOD	SHILOH	MURPHY
SEARS	MARTY	KITE	BAKER	RAY

Shiloh

DEER	SUNDAY	HERMIE	JUDD	SEARS
PRESTON	MA	RAY	NAYLOR	SCRAM
CONTRACT	SNAKES	FREE SPACE	WALLACE	HOWARD
KITE	MARTY	WVA	LAW	ALLERGIC
BAKER	BECKY	ELEVEN	FEEBLE	DAVID

Shiloh

MURPHY	LIES	PET	SHILOH	YELPS
SQUASH	PEN	BEAGLE	DAVID	FEEBLE
ELEVEN	BECKY	FREE SPACE	ALLERGIC	LAW
WVA	MARTY	KITE	HOWARD	WALLACE
BLOOD	SNAKES	CONTRACT	SCRAM	NAYLOR

Shiloh

PRESTON	ELEVEN	BAKER	YELPS	KITE
LIES	SUNDAY	BECKY	PEN	MURPHY
DEER	SQUASH	FREE SPACE	SHILOH	MARTY
CONTRACT	SCRAM	HERMIE	MA	FEEBLE
WVA	LAW	HOWARD	ALLERGIC	BEAGLE

Shiloh

NAYLOR	SNAKES	RAY	PET	DAVID
SEARS	JUDD	WALLACE	BEAGLE	ALLERGIC
HOWARD	LAW	FREE SPACE	FEEBLE	MA
HERMIE	SCRAM	CONTRACT	MARTY	SHILOH
BLOOD	SQUASH	DEER	MURPHY	PEN

Shiloh

JUDD	DEER	WALLACE	BAKER	SQUASH
LAW	MA	CONTRACT	HOWARD	BLOOD
HERMIE	PRESTON	FREE SPACE	LIES	KITE
SEARS	SHILOH	WVA	PET	MARTY
PEN	ALLERGIC	YELPS	SNAKES	BEAGLE

Shiloh

RAY	MURPHY	SUNDAY	FEEBLE	DAVID
BECKY	ELEVEN	SCRAM	BEAGLE	SNAKES
YELPS	ALLERGIC	FREE SPACE	MARTY	PET
WVA	SHILOH	SEARS	KITE	LIES
NAYLOR	PRESTON	HERMIE	BLOOD	HOWARD

Shiloh

NAYLOR	CONTRACT	MA	ELEVEN	MARTY
LAW	FEEBLE	SUNDAY	ALLERGIC	BECKY
WVA	YELPS	FREE SPACE	LIES	SQUASH
DAVID	PET	BLOOD	SNAKES	JUDD
DEER	HERMIE	MURPHY	RAY	PEN

Shiloh

BAKER	SHILOH	KITE	WALLACE	SEARS
SCRAM	HOWARD	PRESTON	PEN	RAY
MURPHY	HERMIE	FREE SPACE	JUDD	SNAKES
BLOOD	PET	DAVID	SQUASH	LIES
BEAGLE	YELPS	WVA	BECKY	ALLERGIC

Shiloh

BECKY	SCRAM	PEN	JUDD	SQUASH
PRESTON	BLOOD	ELEVEN	BAKER	ALLERGIC
MA	LIES	FREE SPACE	MARTY	PET
NAYLOR	SNAKES	WALLACE	DEER	SUNDAY
SEARS	SHILOH	CONTRACT	FEEBLE	KITE

Shiloh

MURPHY	HOWARD	LAW	RAY	YELPS
DAVID	BEAGLE	HERMIE	KITE	FEEBLE
CONTRACT	SHILOH	FREE SPACE	SUNDAY	DEER
WALLACE	SNAKES	NAYLOR	PET	MARTY
WVA	LIES	MA	ALLERGIC	BAKER

Shiloh Vocabulary Word List

No.	Word	Clue/Definition
1.	ABANDONED	Deserted; forsaken
2.	ALLERGIC	Highly sensitive to something physically
3.	ANTIBIOTICS	Substances used to treat infectious diseases
4.	BATS	Flutters
5.	BAWLING	Sobbing loudly; crying; wailing
6.	BLACKMAIL	Get by threatening
7.	BOLDNESS	Fearlessness and daring
8.	CHEAP	At low cost; inexpensive
9.	CLATTER	Din; racket; noise
10.	CLINKING	Making a light, sharp ringing sound
11.	DEVILMENT	Mischief; annoyance
12.	ENTHUSIASM	Excitement or interest for or in something
13.	ENVY	Resentment caused by desire for another's possessions
14.	FEEBLE	Weak
15.	GRISTMILL	Place where grain is ground
16.	GROVELING	Cringing
17.	HARM	Wrong
18.	INVESTIGATOR	Person who inquires or examines
19.	JUBILATION	A joyful celebration
20.	LONELY	Sad at being alone
21.	LOPING	Running easily
22.	MAZE	Network of interconnecting pathways
23.	MISTREATED	Abused
24.	NUDGE	Gentle push
25.	NUMB	Unable to feel normally
26.	OBLIGED	Obligated; grateful
27.	OUTRIGHT	Complete
28.	PET	Animal kept for amusement or companionship
29.	QUAIL	Small, chicken-like game bird
30.	REHEARSED	Practiced
31.	ROOTED	Firmly established; set
32.	SCOLDING	Reprimanding; nagging
33.	SCRAM	Get out; Go away
34.	SHRUGS	Raises shoulders
35.	SLOGS	Walks in a slow, labored way
36.	SLUMP	Fall; sink; droop
37.	SOMERSAULT	Acrobatic stunt in which the body rolls in a circle
38.	SPOILING	Rotting; decaying
39.	SQUARE	Honest; direct
40.	STRAY	Lost; wandering
41.	STUMPED	Puzzled; baffled
42.	SUSPICIONS	Hints; feelings of distrust
43.	SYMPATHY	Pity or sorrow for distress of another
44.	TENSE	Tightly stretched
45.	THRUSTING	Shoving
46.	TRACE	Visual mark or sign
47.	TREMBLING	Shaking from fear or excitement
48.	TUCKERED	Tired
49.	VET	Person who gives medical care to animals
50.	WINCE	Move involuntarily, as in pain
51.	WITNESS	Someone who signs a document to make it authentic

Shiloh Vocabulary Word List

No.	Word	Clue/Definition
52.	YANK	Pull with sudden force
53.	YELP	Short, sharp bark or cry
54.	ZIGZAGGING	Making a series of sharp turns

Shiloh Vocabulary Fill In The Blanks 1

_____ 1. Sad at being alone

_____ 2. Sobbing loudly; crying; wailing

_____ 3. Unable to feel normally

_____ 4. Raises shoulders

_____ 5. Acrobatic stunt in which the body rolls in a circle

_____ 6. Animal kept for amusement or companionship

_____ 7. Resentment caused by desire for another's possessions

_____ 8. Complete

_____ 9. Get by threatening

_____ 10. Someone who signs a document to make it authentic

_____ 11. Person who gives medical care to animals

_____ 12. Honest; direct

_____ 13. Making a series of sharp turns

_____ 14. Flutters

_____ 15. At low cost; inexpensive

_____ 16. Abused

_____ 17. Visual mark or sign

_____ 18. Din; racket; noise

_____ 19. Practiced

_____ 20. Running easily

Shiloh Vocabulary Fill In The Blanks 1 Answer Key

LONELY	1.	Sad at being alone
BAWLING	2.	Sobbing loudly; crying; wailing
NUMB	3.	Unable to feel normally
SHRUGS	4.	Raises shoulders
SOMERSAULT	5.	Acrobatic stunt in which the body rolls in a circle
PET	6.	Animal kept for amusement or companionship
ENVY	7.	Resentment caused by desire for another's possessions
OUTRIGHT	8.	Complete
BLACKMAIL	9.	Get by threatening
WITNESS	10.	Someone who signs a document to make it authentic
VET	11.	Person who gives medical care to animals
SQUARE	12.	Honest; direct
ZIGZAGGING	13.	Making a series of sharp turns
BATS	14.	Flutters
CHEAP	15.	At low cost; inexpensive
MISTREATED	16.	Abused
TRACE	17.	Visual mark or sign
CLATTER	18.	Din; racket; noise
REHEARSED	19.	Practiced
LOPING	20.	Running easily

Shiloh Vocabulary Fill In The Blanks 2

_____ 1. Reprimanding; nagging

_____ 2. At low cost; inexpensive

_____ 3. Din; racket; noise

_____ 4. Deserted; forsaken

_____ 5. Place where grain is ground

_____ 6. Walks in a slow, labored way

_____ 7. Lost; wandering

_____ 8. Unable to feel normally

_____ 9. Tired

_____ 10. Visual mark or sign

_____ 11. Tightly stretched

_____ 12. Gentle push

_____ 13. Someone who signs a document to make it authentic

_____ 14. Puzzled; baffled

_____ 15. Hints; feelings of distrust

_____ 16. Complete

_____ 17. Weak

_____ 18. Get out; Go away

_____ 19. Excitement or interest for or in something

_____ 20. Honest; direct

Shiloh Vocabulary Fill In The Blanks 2 Answer Key

SCOLDING	1. Reprimanding; nagging
CHEAP	2. At low cost; inexpensive
CLATTER	3. Din; racket; noise
ABANDONED	4. Deserted; forsaken
GRISTMILL	5. Place where grain is ground
SLOGS	6. Walks in a slow, labored way
STRAY	7. Lost; wandering
NUMB	8. Unable to feel normally
TUCKERED	9. Tired
TRACE	10. Visual mark or sign
TENSE	11. Tightly stretched
NUDGE	12. Gentle push
WITNESS	13. Someone who signs a document to make it authentic
STUMPED	14. Puzzled; baffled
SUSPICIONS	15. Hints; feelings of distrust
OUTRIGHT	16. Complete
FEEBLE	17. Weak
SCRAM	18. Get out; Go away
ENTHUSIASM	19. Excitement or interest for or in something
SQUARE	20. Honest; direct

Shiloh Vocabulary Fill In The Blanks 3

_____ 1. Running easily

_____ 2. Substances used to treat infectious diseases

_____ 3. Cringing

_____ 4. Walks in a slow, labored way

_____ 5. Pity or sorrow for distress of another

_____ 6. Excitement or interest for or in something

_____ 7. Network of interconnecting pathways

_____ 8. Making a light, sharp ringing sound

_____ 9. Gentle push

_____ 10. Rotting; decaying

_____ 11. Practiced

_____ 12. Deserted; forsaken

_____ 13. Mischief; annoyance

_____ 14. Animal kept for amusement or companionship

_____ 15. Shoving

_____ 16. Weak

_____ 17. Abused

_____ 18. Place where grain is ground

_____ 19. Firmly established; set

_____ 20. Tired

Shiloh Vocabulary Fill In The Blanks 3 Answer Key

LOPING	1. Running easily
ANTIBIOTICS	2. Substances used to treat infectious diseases
GROVELING	3. Cringing
SLOGS	4. Walks in a slow, labored way
SYMPATHY	5. Pity or sorrow for distress of another
ENTHUSIASM	6. Excitement or interest for or in something
MAZE	7. Network of interconnecting pathways
CLINKING	8. Making a light, sharp ringing sound
NUDGE	9. Gentle push
SPOILING	10. Rotting; decaying
REHEARSED	11. Practiced
ABANDONED	12. Deserted; forsaken
DEVILMENT	13. Mischief; annoyance
PET	14. Animal kept for amusement or companionship
THRUSTING	15. Shoving
FEEBLE	16. Weak
MISTREATED	17. Abused
GRISTMILL	18. Place where grain is ground
ROOTED	19. Firmly established; set
TUCKERED	20. Tired

Shiloh Vocabulary Fill In The Blanks 4

_____ 1. Pull with sudden force

_____ 2. Din; racket; noise

_____ 3. Someone who signs a document to make it authentic

_____ 4. Visual mark or sign

_____ 5. Get by threatening

_____ 6. Cringing

_____ 7. Shaking from fear or excitement

_____ 8. Reprimanding; nagging

_____ 9. Tightly stretched

_____ 10. Fearlessness and daring

_____ 11. Flutters

_____ 12. Sobbing loudly; crying; wailing

_____ 13. Shoving

_____ 14. Lost; wandering

_____ 15. Resentment caused by desire for another's possessions

_____ 16. Obligated; grateful

_____ 17. Puzzled; baffled

_____ 18. Making a light, sharp ringing sound

_____ 19. Unable to feel normally

_____ 20. Practiced

Shiloh Vocabulary Fill In The Blanks 4 Answer Key

YANK	1.	Pull with sudden force
CLATTER	2.	Din; racket; noise
WITNESS	3.	Someone who signs a document to make it authentic
TRACE	4.	Visual mark or sign
BLACKMAIL	5.	Get by threatening
GROVELING	6.	Cringing
TREMBLING	7.	Shaking from fear or excitement
SCOLDING	8.	Reprimanding; nagging
TENSE	9.	Tightly stretched
BOLDNESS	10.	Fearlessness and daring
BATS	11.	Flutters
BAWLING	12.	Sobbing loudly; crying; wailing
THRUSTING	13.	Shoving
STRAY	14.	Lost; wandering
ENVY	15.	Resentment caused by desire for another's possessions
OBLIGED	16.	Obligated; grateful
STUMPED	17.	Puzzled; baffled
CLINKING	18.	Making a light, sharp ringing sound
NUMB	19.	Unable to feel normally
REHEARSED	20.	Practiced

Shiloh Vocabulary Matching 1

___ 1. WINCE   A. Puzzled; baffled
___ 2. INVESTIGATOR   B. Reprimanding; nagging
___ 3. SYMPATHY   C. Tired
___ 4. ENVY   D. Honest; direct
___ 5. TUCKERED   E. Making a series of sharp turns
___ 6. CLINKING   F. Get out; Go away
___ 7. BAWLING   G. Acrobatic stunt in which the body rolls in a circle
___ 8. SQUARE   H. Weak
___ 9. BOLDNESS   I. Person who inquires or examines
___10. ZIGZAGGING   J. Move involuntarily, as in pain
___11. SPOILING   K. At low cost; inexpensive
___12. CHEAP   L. Sobbing loudly; crying; wailing
___13. BLACKMAIL   M. Rotting; decaying
___14. SCOLDING   N. Practiced
___15. QUAIL   O. Get by threatening
___16. STRAY   P. Pity or sorrow for distress of another
___17. PET   Q. Lost; wandering
___18. SHRUGS   R. Raises shoulders
___19. DEVILMENT   S. Fearlessness and daring
___20. SCRAM   T. Small, chicken-like game bird
___21. SOMERSAULT   U. Sad at being alone
___22. STUMPED   V. Mischief; annoyance
___23. REHEARSED   W. Animal kept for amusement or companionship
___24. FEEBLE   X. Resentment caused by desire for another's possessions
___25. LONELY   Y. Making a light, sharp ringing sound

Shiloh Vocabulary Matching 1 Answer Key

J - 1. WINCE	A.	Puzzled; baffled
I - 2. INVESTIGATOR	B.	Reprimanding; nagging
P - 3. SYMPATHY	C.	Tired
X - 4. ENVY	D.	Honest; direct
C - 5. TUCKERED	E.	Making a series of sharp turns
Y - 6. CLINKING	F.	Get out; Go away
L - 7. BAWLING	G.	Acrobatic stunt in which the body rolls in a circle
D - 8. SQUARE	H.	Weak
S - 9. BOLDNESS	I.	Person who inquires or examines
E - 10. ZIGZAGGING	J.	Move involuntarily, as in pain
M - 11. SPOILING	K.	At low cost; inexpensive
K - 12. CHEAP	L.	Sobbing loudly; crying; wailing
O - 13. BLACKMAIL	M.	Rotting; decaying
B - 14. SCOLDING	N.	Practiced
T - 15. QUAIL	O.	Get by threatening
Q - 16. STRAY	P.	Pity or sorrow for distress of another
W - 17. PET	Q.	Lost; wandering
R - 18. SHRUGS	R.	Raises shoulders
V - 19. DEVILMENT	S.	Fearlessness and daring
F - 20. SCRAM	T.	Small, chicken-like game bird
G - 21. SOMERSAULT	U.	Sad at being alone
A - 22. STUMPED	V.	Mischief; annoyance
N - 23. REHEARSED	W.	Animal kept for amusement or companionship
H - 24. FEEBLE	X.	Resentment caused by desire for another's possessions
U - 25. LONELY	Y.	Making a light, sharp ringing sound

Shiloh Vocabulary Matching 2

___ 1. HARM   A. Running easily
___ 2. QUAIL   B. Get by threatening
___ 3. BAWLING   C. Practiced
___ 4. WITNESS   D. Network of interconnecting pathways
___ 5. BATS   E. Lost; wandering
___ 6. PET   F. Making a series of sharp turns
___ 7. ZIGZAGGING   G. Reprimanding; nagging
___ 8. LOPING   H. Small, chicken-like game bird
___ 9. JUBILATION   I. Din; racket; noise
___10. SCOLDING   J. A joyful celebration
___11. INVESTIGATOR   K. Sobbing loudly; crying; wailing
___12. BLACKMAIL   L. Wrong
___13. ENTHUSIASM   M. Cringing
___14. CLATTER   N. Flutters
___15. THRUSTING   O. Sad at being alone
___16. DEVILMENT   P. Shoving
___17. REHEARSED   Q. Weak
___18. GROVELING   R. Excitement or interest for or in something
___19. MAZE   S. Person who inquires or examines
___20. STRAY   T. Someone who signs a document to make it authentic
___21. NUMB   U. Tired
___22. ENVY   V. Mischief; annoyance
___23. LONELY   W. Unable to feel normally
___24. TUCKERED   X. Animal kept for amusement or companionship
___25. FEEBLE   Y. Resentment caused by desire for another's possessions

Shiloh Vocabulary Matching 2 Answer Key

L - 1.	HARM	A. Running easily
H - 2.	QUAIL	B. Get by threatening
K - 3.	BAWLING	C. Practiced
T - 4.	WITNESS	D. Network of interconnecting pathways
N - 5.	BATS	E. Lost; wandering
X - 6.	PET	F. Making a series of sharp turns
F - 7.	ZIGZAGGING	G. Reprimanding; nagging
A - 8.	LOPING	H. Small, chicken-like game bird
J - 9.	JUBILATION	I. Din; racket; noise
G -10.	SCOLDING	J. A joyful celebration
S -11.	INVESTIGATOR	K. Sobbing loudly; crying; wailing
B -12.	BLACKMAIL	L. Wrong
R -13.	ENTHUSIASM	M. Cringing
I -14.	CLATTER	N. Flutters
P -15.	THRUSTING	O. Sad at being alone
V -16.	DEVILMENT	P. Shoving
C -17.	REHEARSED	Q. Weak
M -18.	GROVELING	R. Excitement or interest for or in something
D -19.	MAZE	S. Person who inquires or examines
E -20.	STRAY	T. Someone who signs a document to make it authentic
W -21.	NUMB	U. Tired
Y -22.	ENVY	V. Mischief; annoyance
O -23.	LONELY	W. Unable to feel normally
U -24.	TUCKERED	X. Animal kept for amusement or companionship
Q -25.	FEEBLE	Y. Resentment caused by desire for another's possessions

Shiloh Vocabulary Matching 3

___ 1. BOLDNESS A. Person who gives medical care to animals
___ 2. SCOLDING B. Din; racket; noise
___ 3. VET C. Resentment caused by desire for another's possessions
___ 4. CLATTER D. Lost; wandering
___ 5. ENTHUSIASM E. Gentle push
___ 6. SLUMP F. Shoving
___ 7. YANK G. Fall; sink; droop
___ 8. TRACE H. Visual mark or sign
___ 9. HARM I. Hints; feelings of distrust
___10. REHEARSED J. Reprimanding; nagging
___11. WINCE K. Shaking from fear or excitement
___12. ENVY L. Pull with sudden force
___13. BLACKMAIL M. Move involuntarily, as in pain
___14. PET N. Practiced
___15. SUSPICIONS O. Tightly stretched
___16. SPOILING P. Animal kept for amusement or companionship
___17. TENSE Q. Running easily
___18. SHRUGS R. Wrong
___19. NUDGE S. Get by threatening
___20. BAWLING T. Sobbing loudly; crying; wailing
___21. STRAY U. Network of interconnecting pathways
___22. TREMBLING V. Excitement or interest for or in something
___23. THRUSTING W. Fearlessness and daring
___24. LOPING X. Raises shoulders
___25. MAZE Y. Rotting; decaying

Shiloh Vocabulary Matching 3 Answer Key

W - 1.	BOLDNESS	A. Person who gives medical care to animals
J - 2.	SCOLDING	B. Din; racket; noise
A - 3.	VET	C. Resentment caused by desire for another's possessions
B - 4.	CLATTER	D. Lost; wandering
V - 5.	ENTHUSIASM	E. Gentle push
G - 6.	SLUMP	F. Shoving
L - 7.	YANK	G. Fall; sink; droop
H - 8.	TRACE	H. Visual mark or sign
R - 9.	HARM	I. Hints; feelings of distrust
N - 10.	REHEARSED	J. Reprimanding; nagging
M - 11.	WINCE	K. Shaking from fear or excitement
C - 12.	ENVY	L. Pull with sudden force
S - 13.	BLACKMAIL	M. Move involuntarily, as in pain
P - 14.	PET	N. Practiced
I - 15.	SUSPICIONS	O. Tightly stretched
Y - 16.	SPOILING	P. Animal kept for amusement or companionship
O - 17.	TENSE	Q. Running easily
X - 18.	SHRUGS	R. Wrong
E - 19.	NUDGE	S. Get by threatening
T - 20.	BAWLING	T. Sobbing loudly; crying; wailing
D - 21.	STRAY	U. Network of interconnecting pathways
K - 22.	TREMBLING	V. Excitement or interest for or in something
F - 23.	THRUSTING	W. Fearlessness and daring
Q - 24.	LOPING	X. Raises shoulders
U - 25.	MAZE	Y. Rotting; decaying

Shiloh Vocabulary Matching 4

___ 1. VET   A. Mischief; annoyance
___ 2. ENTHUSIASM   B. Person who inquires or examines
___ 3. REHEARSED   C. Rotting; decaying
___ 4. ABANDONED   D. Sad at being alone
___ 5. DEVILMENT   E. Get out; Go away
___ 6. SCRAM   F. Pity or sorrow for distress of another
___ 7. CLATTER   G. Flutters
___ 8. NUMB   H. Deserted; forsaken
___ 9. LONELY   I. Fearlessness and daring
___10. HARM   J. Place where grain is ground
___11. SLUMP   K. Din; racket; noise
___12. CLINKING   L. Unable to feel normally
___13. ENVY   M. Fall; sink; droop
___14. TREMBLING   N. Making a light, sharp ringing sound
___15. PET   O. Hints; feelings of distrust
___16. INVESTIGATOR   P. Abused
___17. TUCKERED   Q. Visual mark or sign
___18. BOLDNESS   R. Practiced
___19. GRISTMILL   S. Person who gives medical care to animals
___20. SPOILING   T. Tired
___21. SYMPATHY   U. Wrong
___22. TRACE   V. Resentment caused by desire for another's possessions
___23. SUSPICIONS   W. Excitement or interest for or in something
___24. BATS   X. Animal kept for amusement or companionship
___25. MISTREATED   Y. Shaking from fear or excitement

Shiloh Vocabulary Matching 4 Answer Key

S - 1. VET	A.	Mischief; annoyance
W - 2. ENTHUSIASM	B.	Person who inquires or examines
R - 3. REHEARSED	C.	Rotting; decaying
H - 4. ABANDONED	D.	Sad at being alone
A - 5. DEVILMENT	E.	Get out; Go away
E - 6. SCRAM	F.	Pity or sorrow for distress of another
K - 7. CLATTER	G.	Flutters
L - 8. NUMB	H.	Deserted; forsaken
D - 9. LONELY	I.	Fearlessness and daring
U - 10. HARM	J.	Place where grain is ground
M - 11. SLUMP	K.	Din; racket; noise
N - 12. CLINKING	L.	Unable to feel normally
V - 13. ENVY	M.	Fall; sink; droop
Y - 14. TREMBLING	N.	Making a light, sharp ringing sound
X - 15. PET	O.	Hints; feelings of distrust
B - 16. INVESTIGATOR	P.	Abused
T - 17. TUCKERED	Q.	Visual mark or sign
I - 18. BOLDNESS	R.	Practiced
J - 19. GRISTMILL	S.	Person who gives medical care to animals
C - 20. SPOILING	T.	Tired
F - 21. SYMPATHY	U.	Wrong
Q - 22. TRACE	V.	Resentment caused by desire for another's possessions
O - 23. SUSPICIONS	W.	Excitement or interest for or in something
G - 24. BATS	X.	Animal kept for amusement or companionship
P - 25. MISTREATED	Y.	Shaking from fear or excitement

Shiloh Vocabulary Magic Squares 1

Match the definition with the vocabulary word. Put your answers in the magic squares below. When your answers are correct, all columns and rows will add to the same number.

A. LOPING
B. BATS
C. CLINKING
D. CHEAP
E. NUMB
F. SCRAM
G. OBLIGED
H. ANTIBIOTICS
I. SYMPATHY
J. TENSE
K. FEEBLE
L. SUSPICIONS
M. BAWLING
N. SCOLDING
O. YELP
P. HARM

1. Substances used to treat infectious diseases
2. Sobbing loudly; crying; wailing
3. Flutters
4. Weak
5. Tightly stretched
6. Making a light, sharp ringing sound
7. Wrong
8. Unable to feel normally
9. Short, sharp bark or cry
10. Get out; Go away
11. Pity or sorrow for distress of another
12. At low cost; inexpensive
13. Running easily
14. Hints; feelings of distrust
15. Obligated; grateful
16. Reprimanding; nagging

A=	B=	C=	D=
E=	F=	G=	H=
I=	J=	K=	L=
M=	N=	O=	P=

Shiloh Vocabulary Magic Squares 1 Answer Key

Match the definition with the vocabulary word. Put your answers in the magic squares below. When your answers are correct, all columns and rows will add to the same number.

A. LOPING
B. BATS
C. CLINKING
D. CHEAP

E. NUMB
F. SCRAM
G. OBLIGED
H. ANTIBIOTICS

I. SYMPATHY
J. TENSE
K. FEEBLE
L. SUSPICIONS

M. BAWLING
N. SCOLDING
O. YELP
P. HARM

1. Substances used to treat infectious diseases
2. Sobbing loudly; crying; wailing
3. Flutters
4. Weak
5. Tightly stretched
6. Making a light, sharp ringing sound
7. Wrong
8. Unable to feel normally
9. Short, sharp bark or cry
10. Get out; Go away
11. Pity or sorrow for distress of another
12. At low cost; inexpensive
13. Running easily
14. Hints; feelings of distrust
15. Obligated; grateful
16. Reprimanding; nagging

A=13	B=3	C=6	D=12
E=8	F=10	G=15	H=1
I=11	J=5	K=4	L=14
M=2	N=16	O=9	P=7

Shiloh Vocabulary Magic Squares 2

Match the definition with the vocabulary word. Put your answers in the magic squares below. When your answers are correct, all columns and rows will add to the same number.

A. CLATTER
B. BLACKMAIL
C. STRAY
D. QUAIL
E. YELP
F. SCOLDING
G. ENVY
H. STUMPED
I. GRISTMILL
J. CLINKING
K. SHRUGS
L. BOLDNESS
M. INVESTIGATOR
N. TENSE
O. REHEARSED
P. TREMBLING

1. Practiced
2. Small, chicken-like game bird
3. Making a light, sharp ringing sound
4. Short, sharp bark or cry
5. Place where grain is ground
6. Reprimanding; nagging
7. Shaking from fear or excitement
8. Lost; wandering
9. Puzzled; baffled
10. Raises shoulders
11. Din; racket; noise
12. Tightly stretched
13. Get by threatening
14. Person who inquires or examines
15. Resentment caused by desire for another's possessions
16. Fearlessness and daring

A=	B=	C=	D=
E=	F=	G=	H=
I=	J=	K=	L=
M=	N=	O=	P=

Shiloh Vocabulary Magic Squares 2 Answer Key

Match the definition with the vocabulary word. Put your answers in the magic squares below. When your answers are correct, all columns and rows will add to the same number.

A. CLATTER
B. BLACKMAIL
C. STRAY
D. QUAIL
E. YELP
F. SCOLDING
G. ENVY
H. STUMPED
I. GRISTMILL
J. CLINKING
K. SHRUGS
L. BOLDNESS
M. INVESTIGATOR
N. TENSE
O. REHEARSED
P. TREMBLING

1. Practiced
2. Small, chicken-like game bird
3. Making a light, sharp ringing sound
4. Short, sharp bark or cry
5. Place where grain is ground
6. Reprimanding; nagging
7. Shaking from fear or excitement
8. Lost; wandering
9. Puzzled; baffled
10. Raises shoulders
11. Din; racket; noise
12. Tightly stretched
13. Get by threatening
14. Person who inquires or examines
15. Resentment caused by desire for another's possessions
16. Fearlessness and daring

A=11	B=13	C=8	D=2
E=4	F=6	G=15	H=9
I=5	J=3	K=10	L=16
M=14	N=12	O=1	P=7

Shiloh Vocabulary Magic Squares 3

Match the definition with the vocabulary word. Put your answers in the magic squares below. When your answers are correct, all columns and rows will add to the same number.

A. SHRUGS
B. BOLDNESS
C. OUTRIGHT
D. OBLIGED
E. WINCE
F. PET
G. SLUMP
H. TREMBLING
I. ZIGZAGGING
J. DEVILMENT
K. LOPING
L. NUDGE
M. SQUARE
N. GROVELING
O. YELP
P. ANTIBIOTICS

1. Fearlessness and daring
2. Fall; sink; droop
3. Running easily
4. Cringing
5. Honest; direct
6. Gentle push
7. Shaking from fear or excitement
8. Raises shoulders
9. Substances used to treat infectious diseases
10. Making a series of sharp turns
11. Move involuntarily, as in pain
12. Obligated; grateful
13. Complete
14. Animal kept for amusement or companionship
15. Mischief; annoyance
16. Short, sharp bark or cry

A=	B=	C=	D=
E=	F=	G=	H=
I=	J=	K=	L=
M=	N=	O=	P=

83
Copyrighted

Shiloh Vocabulary Magic Squares 3 Answer Key

Match the definition with the vocabulary word. Put your answers in the magic squares below. When your answers are correct, all columns and rows will add to the same number.

A. SHRUGS
B. BOLDNESS
C. OUTRIGHT
D. OBLIGED
E. WINCE
F. PET
G. SLUMP
H. TREMBLING
I. ZIGZAGGING
J. DEVILMENT
K. LOPING
L. NUDGE
M. SQUARE
N. GROVELING
O. YELP
P. ANTIBIOTICS

1. Fearlessness and daring
2. Fall; sink; droop
3. Running easily
4. Cringing
5. Honest; direct
6. Gentle push
7. Shaking from fear or excitement
8. Raises shoulders
9. Substances used to treat infectious diseases
10. Making a series of sharp turns
11. Move involuntarily, as in pain
12. Obligated; grateful
13. Complete
14. Animal kept for amusement or companionship
15. Mischief; annoyance
16. Short, sharp bark or cry

A=8	B=1	C=13	D=12
E=11	F=14	G=2	H=7
I=10	J=15	K=3	L=6
M=5	N=4	O=16	P=9

Shiloh Vocabulary Magic Squares 4

Match the definition with the vocabulary word. Put your answers in the magic squares below. When your answers are correct, all columns and rows will add to the same number.

A. ABANDONED   E. LOPING   I. CHEAP   M. MAZE
B. BATS   F. QUAIL   J. PET   N. CLATTER
C. ANTIBIOTICS G. INVESTIGATOR K. MISTREATED   O. SLOGS
D. SYMPATHY   H. JUBILATION   L. BLACKMAIL   P. SHRUGS

1. Deserted; forsaken
2. Din; racket; noise
3. Animal kept for amusement or companionship
4. Running easily
5. Person who inquires or examines
6. Get by threatening
7. Raises shoulders
8. Substances used to treat infectious diseases
9. Walks in a slow, labored way
10. Pity or sorrow for distress of another
11. A joyful celebration
12. Abused
13. At low cost; inexpensive
14. Small, chicken-like game bird
15. Flutters
16. Network of interconnecting pathways

A=	B=	C=	D=
E=	F=	G=	H=
I=	J=	K=	L=
M=	N=	O=	P=

Shiloh Vocabulary Magic Squares 4 Answer Key

Match the definition with the vocabulary word. Put your answers in the magic squares below. When your answers are correct, all columns and rows will add to the same number.

A. ABANDONED
B. BATS
C. ANTIBIOTICS
D. SYMPATHY
E. LOPING
F. QUAIL
G. INVESTIGATOR
H. JUBILATION
I. CHEAP
J. PET
K. MISTREATED
L. BLACKMAIL
M. MAZE
N. CLATTER
O. SLOGS
P. SHRUGS

1. Deserted; forsaken
2. Din; racket; noise
3. Animal kept for amusement or companionship
4. Running easily
5. Person who inquires or examines
6. Get by threatening
7. Raises shoulders
8. Substances used to treat infectious diseases
9. Walks in a slow, labored way
10. Pity or sorrow for distress of another
11. A joyful celebration
12. Abused
13. At low cost; inexpensive
14. Small, chicken-like game bird
15. Flutters
16. Network of interconnecting pathways

A=1	B=15	C=8	D=10
E=4	F=14	G=5	H=11
I=13	J=3	K=12	L=6
M=16	N=2	O=9	P=7

Shiloh Vocabulary Word Search 1

```
T X T Y M Y W Y P J U B I L A T I O N B
R E X G J I H F C C L Z S Q U A R E R H
E C N D G T S P Y A E N T H U S I A S M
H S L S A S F T C D E V I L M E N T V S
E Q Z P E T L K R Z E Y X O B L I G E D
A X M Q C R M O L E Z A P V D K N W N H
R Y D V N A B L G P A R E P Y I T M U Z
S U S P I C I O N S M T U C K E R E D W
E O S L W E H N U L H S E N P A L E G N
D J M G W R B E V T P R I D H Y P P E G
K X W E Z I A L A V R L U V J M A A B F
Y A N K R R T Y F P C I W G U S L B A L
Y L G D M S S N E S Z R G T S P L A W M
K F O A R L A Z E X Q O S H W O E N L J
J K R P W L N U B S K O N S T I R D I H
X C D J I J M Y L P S T U L F L G O N X
S G K A V N V G E T F E M U T I I N G J
C W U V X N G J H P L D B M Q N C E H Y
T Q B D E B O L D N E S S P Q G L D W Z
```

A joyful celebration (10)
Abused (10)
Acrobatic stunt in which the body rolls in a circle (10)
Animal kept for amusement or companionship (3)
At low cost; inexpensive (5)
Complete (8)
Deserted; forsaken (9)
Excitement or interest for or in something (10)
Fall; sink; droop (5)
Fearlessness and daring (8)
Firmly established; set (6)
Flutters (4)
Gentle push (5)
Get by threatening (9)
Get out; Go away (5)
Highly sensitive to something physically (8)
Hints; feelings of distrust (10)
Honest; direct (6)
Lost; wandering (5)
Making a light, sharp ringing sound (8)
Mischief; annoyance (9)
Move involuntarily, as in pain (5)
Network of interconnecting pathways (4)

Obligated; grateful (7)
Person who gives medical care to animals (3)
Pity or sorrow for distress of another (8)
Practiced (9)
Pull with sudden force (4)
Puzzled; baffled (7)
Raises shoulders (6)
Resentment caused by desire for another's possessions (4)
Rotting; decaying (8)
Running easily (6)
Sad at being alone (6)
Short, sharp bark or cry (4)
Small, chicken-like game bird (5)
Sobbing loudly; crying; wailing (7)
Someone who signs a document to make it authentic (7)
Tightly stretched (5)
Tired (8)
Unable to feel normally (4)
Visual mark or sign (5)
Walks in a slow, labored way (5)
Weak (6)
Wrong (4)

Shiloh Vocabulary Word Search 1 Answer Key

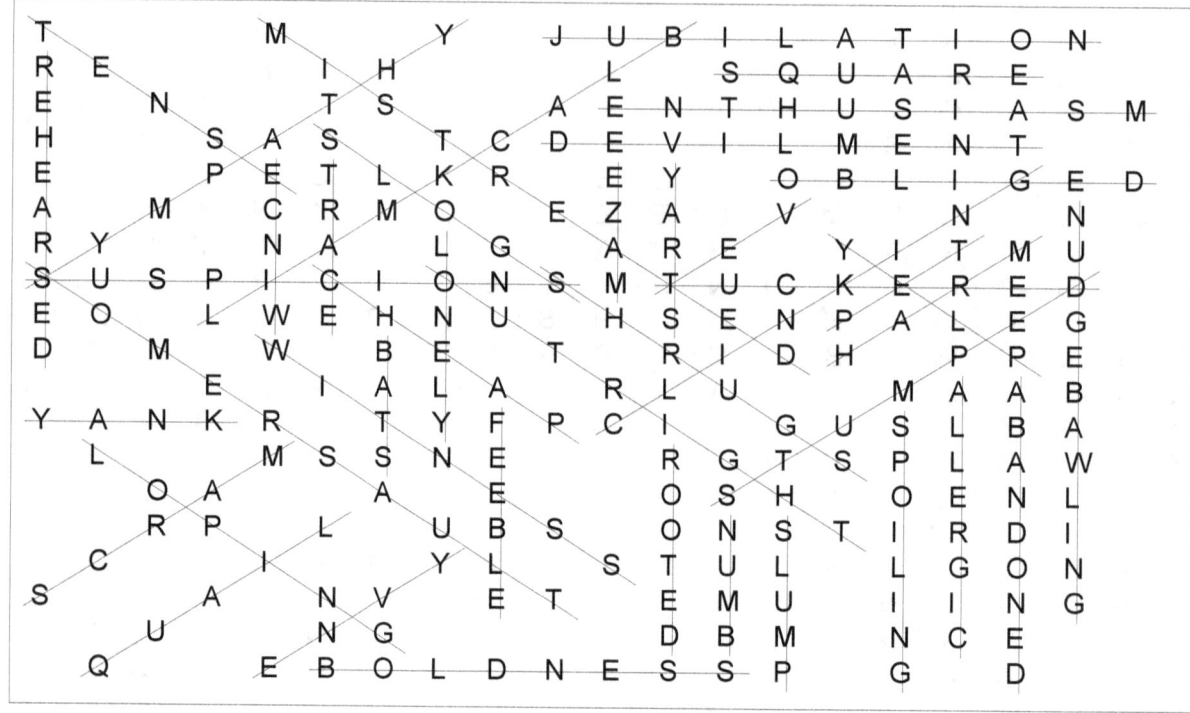

A joyful celebration (10)
Abused (10)
Acrobatic stunt in which the body rolls in a circle (10)
Animal kept for amusement or companionship (3)
At low cost; inexpensive (5)
Complete (8)
Deserted; forsaken (9)
Excitement or interest for or in something (10)
Fall; sink; droop (5)
Fearlessness and daring (8)
Firmly established; set (6)
Flutters (4)
Gentle push (5)
Get by threatening (9)
Get out; Go away (5)
Highly sensitive to something physically (8)
Hints; feelings of distrust (10)
Honest; direct (6)
Lost; wandering (5)
Making a light, sharp ringing sound (8)
Mischief; annoyance (9)
Move involuntarily, as in pain (5)
Network of interconnecting pathways (4)

Obligated; grateful (7)
Person who gives medical care to animals (3)
Pity or sorrow for distress of another (8)
Practiced (9)
Pull with sudden force (4)
Puzzled; baffled (7)
Raises shoulders (6)
Resentment caused by desire for another's possessions (4)
Rotting; decaying (8)
Running easily (6)
Sad at being alone (6)
Short, sharp bark or cry (4)
Small, chicken-like game bird (5)
Sobbing loudly; crying; wailing (7)
Someone who signs a document to make it authentic (7)
Tightly stretched (5)
Tired (8)
Unable to feel normally (4)
Visual mark or sign (5)
Walks in a slow, labored way (5)
Weak (6)
Wrong (4)

Shiloh Vocabulary Word Search 2

```
S S E N D L O B C S S E N T I W Y E S W
R H P R V Y D K A L W L C H H M C N T C
O J R O V Z K H M W I X U X R A O T U G
Q U H U I C H E A P L N N M R R B H M K
U B T A G L G H Z W U I K T P C L U P K
A I R R R S I H E M S H N I N S I S E T
I L F E I M X N B S Y R C G N S G I D M
L A T E H G C B G Q M O L W Z G E A E X
O T T H E E H Z V U P T A I G Z D S R Z
N I S V R B A T R A A T N L D C M E Y
E O F G T U L R C R T G T C L Z G H K B
L N T K N C S E S E H I E E L N X V C V
Y J D Y E Z N T Y E Y T R R I E D D U M
J D M E M K T S I R D S V L M Q N Y T D
R B E L L J S L O N F E E Q T F B V V T
S U S P I C I O N S G V E T S T R A Y J
P M N Z V P T G B R O N G N I D L O C S
B E E V E E P S Z R M I S T R E A T E D
B A T S D N U D G E Y A N K G N I P O L
```

A joyful celebration (10)
Abused (10)
Animal kept for amusement or companionship (3)
At low cost; inexpensive (5)
Complete (8)
Cringing (9)
Din; racket; noise (7)
Excitement or interest for or in something (10)
Fall; sink; droop (5)
Fearlessness and daring (8)
Firmly established; set (6)
Flutters (4)
Gentle push (5)
Get out; Go away (5)
Hints; feelings of distrust (10)
Honest; direct (6)
Lost; wandering (5)
Making a light, sharp ringing sound (8)
Mischief; annoyance (9)
Move involuntarily, as in pain (5)
Network of interconnecting pathways (4)
Obligated; grateful (7)
Person who gives medical care to animals (3)
Person who inquires or examines (12)

Pity or sorrow for distress of another (8)
Place where grain is ground (9)
Practiced (9)
Pull with sudden force (4)
Puzzled; baffled (7)
Raises shoulders (6)
Reprimanding; nagging (8)
Resentment caused by desire for another's possessions (4)
Rotting; decaying (8)
Running easily (6)
Sad at being alone (6)
Short, sharp bark or cry (4)
Shoving (9)
Small, chicken-like game bird (5)
Sobbing loudly; crying; wailing (7)
Someone who signs a document to make it authentic (7)
Tightly stretched (5)
Tired (8)
Unable to feel normally (4)
Visual mark or sign (5)
Walks in a slow, labored way (5)
Weak (6)
Wrong (4)

Shiloh Vocabulary Word Search 2 Answer Key

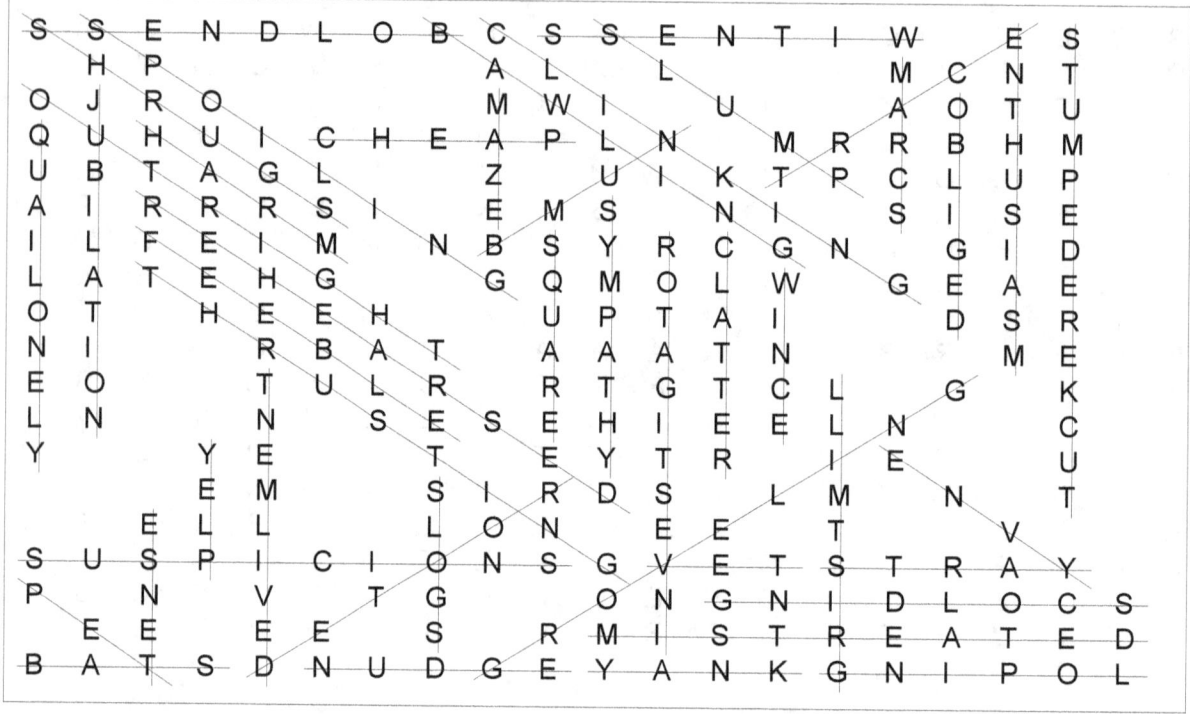

A joyful celebration (10)
Abused (10)
Animal kept for amusement or companionship (3)
At low cost; inexpensive (5)
Complete (8)
Cringing (9)
Din; racket; noise (7)
Excitement or interest for or in something (10)
Fall; sink; droop (5)
Fearlessness and daring (8)
Firmly established; set (6)
Flutters (4)
Gentle push (5)
Get out; Go away (5)
Hints; feelings of distrust (10)
Honest; direct (6)
Lost; wandering (5)
Making a light, sharp ringing sound (8)
Mischief; annoyance (9)
Move involuntarily, as in pain (5)
Network of interconnecting pathways (4)
Obligated; grateful (7)
Person who gives medical care to animals (3)
Person who inquires or examines (12)

Pity or sorrow for distress of another (8)
Place where grain is ground (9)
Practiced (9)
Pull with sudden force (4)
Puzzled; baffled (7)
Raises shoulders (6)
Reprimanding; nagging (8)
Resentment caused by desire for another's possessions (4)
Rotting; decaying (8)
Running easily (6)
Sad at being alone (6)
Short, sharp bark or cry (4)
Shoving (9)
Small, chicken-like game bird (5)
Sobbing loudly; crying; wailing (7)
Someone who signs a document to make it authentic (7)
Tightly stretched (5)
Tired (8)
Unable to feel normally (4)
Visual mark or sign (5)
Walks in a slow, labored way (5)
Weak (6)
Wrong (4)

Shiloh Vocabulary Word Search 3

```
A N T I B I O T I C S G R O V E L I N G
B W E Z X N G M F L Y R S W E R O Q D W
A D N H T B N Q V A M I C I N A N D E X
N R S Q U A I L X T P S O T T U E M V R
D D E W J F L R G T A T L N H Q L P I K
O K T S X F W T L E T M D E U S Y R L Q
N T R A C E A D U R H I I S S C R A M B
E J A D F D B Q D C Y L N S I G G S E K
D T L N T M H T E L K L G V A N M P N P
O B L I G E D M T V Q E D D S I F O T Z
R B E P S K Y B A W K B R Q M L E I S T
E L R B W B K Q E V G N B E C B E L N W
H A G F Q Q A J R Z R U R H D M B I R T
E C I V E B G T T L I D S O A E L N P T
A K C W I N V E S T I G A T O R E G E Q
R M M G I Y V S I F O E Z U U T M V T J
S A S P W N E Y M L S T T A S M E S B B
E I O Y Y N C J S G R R P Y G L P D W G
D L P A D K E E U P I A B A S G U E G B
N C R L L Z P R L G E M M N H W I M D J
D T O S A N H E H H U V F K J B H N P D
S B G M X S Y T C N C L I N K I N G G F
```

ABANDONED	DEVILMENT	MAZE	SCOLDING	TENSE
ALLERGIC	ENTHUSIASM	MISTREATED	SCRAM	TRACE
ANTIBIOTICS	ENVY	NUDGE	SHRUGS	TREMBLING
BATS	FEEBLE	NUMB	SLOGS	TUCKERED
BAWLING	GRISTMILL	OBLIGED	SLUMP	VET
BLACKMAIL	GROVELING	OUTRIGHT	SPOILING	WINCE
BOLDNESS	HARM	PET	SQUARE	WITNESS
CHEAP	INVESTIGATOR	QUAIL	STRAY	YANK
CLATTER	LONELY	REHEARSED	STUMPED	YELP
CLINKING	LOPING	ROOTED	SYMPATHY	ZIGZAGGING

Shiloh Vocabulary Word Search 3 Answer Key

ABANDONED	DEVILMENT	MAZE	SCOLDING	TENSE
ALLERGIC	ENTHUSIASM	MISTREATED	SCRAM	TRACE
ANTIBIOTICS	ENVY	NUDGE	SHRUGS	TREMBLING
BATS	FEEBLE	NUMB	SLOGS	TUCKERED
BAWLING	GRISTMILL	OBLIGED	SLUMP	VET
BLACKMAIL	GROVELING	OUTRIGHT	SPOILING	WINCE
BOLDNESS	HARM	PET	SQUARE	WITNESS
CHEAP	INVESTIGATOR	QUAIL	STRAY	YANK
CLATTER	LONELY	REHEARSED	STUMPED	YELP
CLINKING	LOPING	ROOTED	SYMPATHY	ZIGZAGGING

Shiloh Vocabulary Word Search 4

```
O Z I G Z A G G I N G S Y M P A T H Y V
G U Z L G K H B C S O M E R S A U L T G
R X T H O R R X A N T I B I O T I C S H
I R S R R P L I N V E S T I G A T O R Q
S V H G I Y I C G N I T S U R H T O Z S
T T R G M G H N B V J R M J G N B S Z Y
M Y U N F P H D G Z G E D J X L P C W X
I F G I Q D G T S B T A Z Q I D L O N N
L D S L R G L M T O P T Q G V X Q L K V
L E E E V Z M Q U L L E E W W C S D E N
S N J V S C R A M D L D C L I N K I N G
P O H O I V M D P N B W H G N T G N T D
L D T R Q L E Z E E A J R R C S N G H L
E N Y G H R M V D S W E G R E S C E U W
Y A N K E S N E T S L Q P E T Y G D S J
C B H K V L C T N L I U J A V N E L I S
L A C A E A F L A T N A B N I T U Z A T
A U L V R Y E O S H G I E L O M P B S J
T T B T A M E N L S N L I O P A M E M P
T B R R U R B E O T V O R K E U Z N F J
E X T R Q S L L G V P C J H N A P N V J
R S V S S G E Y S S B R C S M N U D G E
```

ABANDONED	ENTHUSIASM	MISTREATED	SHRUGS	THRUSTING
ALLERGIC	ENVY	NUDGE	SLOGS	TRACE
ANTIBIOTICS	FEEBLE	NUMB	SLUMP	TUCKERED
BATS	GRISTMILL	OBLIGED	SOMERSAULT	VET
BAWLING	GROVELING	OUTRIGHT	SPOILING	WINCE
BOLDNESS	HARM	PET	SQUARE	WITNESS
CHEAP	INVESTIGATOR	QUAIL	STRAY	YANK
CLATTER	LONELY	ROOTED	STUMPED	YELP
CLINKING	LOPING	SCOLDING	SYMPATHY	ZIGZAGGING
DEVILMENT	MAZE	SCRAM	TENSE	

Shiloh Vocabulary Word Search 4 Answer Key

```
O  Z     G  Z  A  G  G  I  N  G  S  Y  M  P  A  T  H  Y
G  U     L              S  O  M  E  R  S  A  U  L  T
R     T  O        P     A  N  T  I  B  I  O  T  I  C  S
I     S  R     P        I  N  V  E  S  T  I  G  A  T  O  R
S     H  R  I  G  H     G  N  I  T  S  U  R  H  T     O
T     R  G     G  H  T           R                 B     S
M     U  N     H  T     G        E                       C
I     G  I        T     S  B     A                 L     O
L     S  L              T  O     T           G           L
L        E  V           U  L  D  E        W  W  C        D
      D  O  O     S  C  R  A  M  D     C  L  I  N  K  I  N  G
      E  N  R     I     D  P  N  B     L  G  N           E
P     N     G     L     E  M     A        R  C  S        N
L     O     K     E     R  N     W        E     Y  G     T
E     D     E  S  N     S  E  T  L  Q  P  E  T  N  D     H
Y  A  N  K  E     N     C  T     I  U  A  V  I  U        U
C  B     H  K     C  A  E  A  F  N  A  B  N  T  P  B     S
L  A     C  A  E  A  R  Y  M  E  A  I  E  L  O  P     M  I
A  U           R     A  U  E  B  S  L  O  P  A  M  E     A
T           T  R     U  G  L  E  L     R  H  N  A  Z  M  S
T                 S  Q  S  E  Y  S  S  P  C  M  N  U  D  G  E
E
R
```

ABANDONED	ENTHUSIASM	MISTREATED	SHRUGS	THRUSTING
ALLERGIC	ENVY	NUDGE	SLOGS	TRACE
ANTIBIOTICS	FEEBLE	NUMB	SLUMP	TUCKERED
BATS	GRISTMILL	OBLIGED	SOMERSAULT	VET
BAWLING	GROVELING	OUTRIGHT	SPOILING	WINCE
BOLDNESS	HARM	PET	SQUARE	WITNESS
CHEAP	INVESTIGATOR	QUAIL	STRAY	YANK
CLATTER	LONELY	ROOTED	STUMPED	YELP
CLINKING	LOPING	SCOLDING	SYMPATHY	ZIGZAGGING
DEVILMENT	MAZE	SCRAM	TENSE	

Shiloh Vocabulary Crossword 1

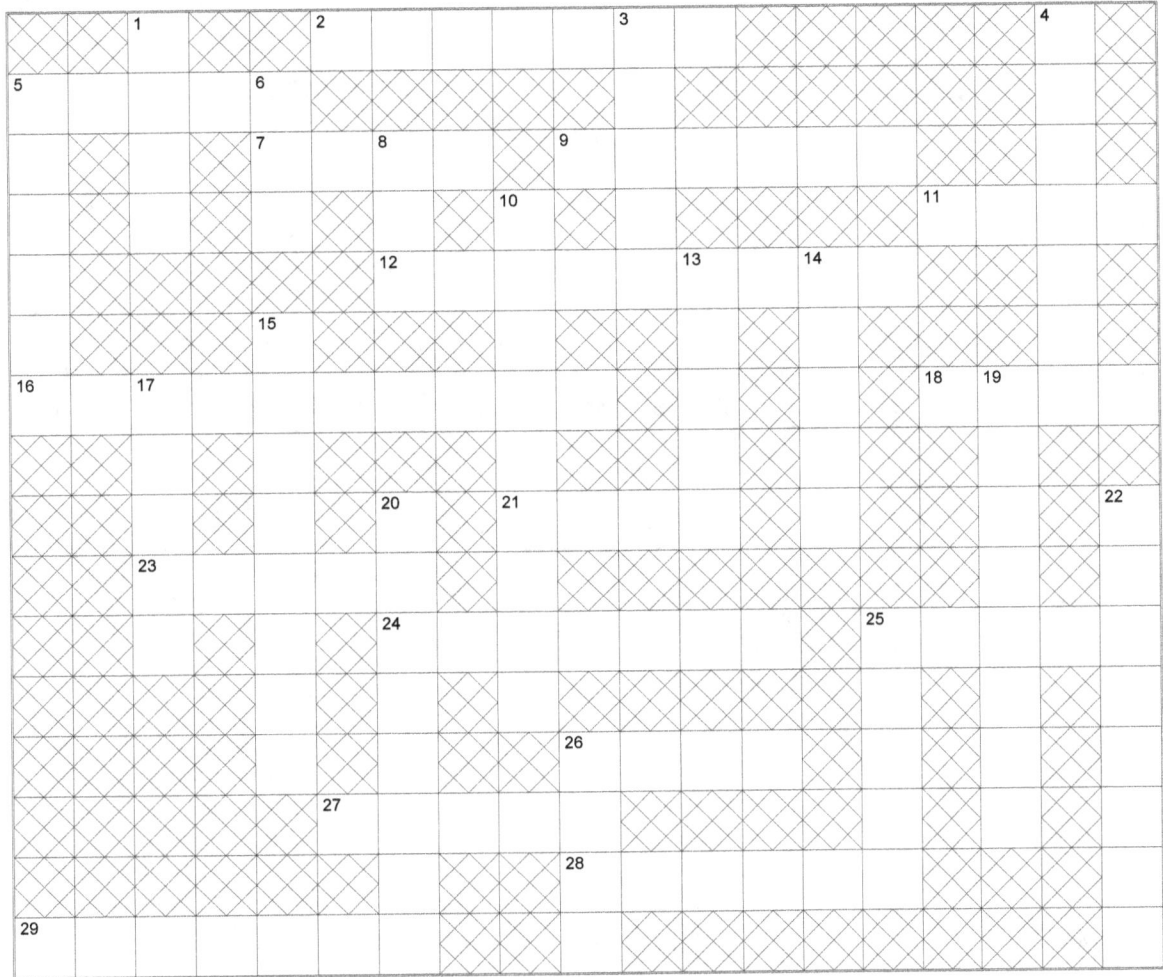

Across
2. Someone who signs a document to make it authentic
5. Fall; sink; droop
7. Resentment caused by desire for another's possessions
9. Firmly established; set
11. Flutters
12. Shoving
16. Excitement or interest for or in something
18. Wrong
21. Network of interconnecting pathways
23. At low cost; inexpensive
24. Obligated; grateful
25. Get out; Go away
26. Pull with sudden force
27. Move involuntarily, as in pain
28. Sad at being alone
29. Sobbing loudly; crying; wailing

Down
1. Unable to feel normally
3. Walks in a slow, labored way
4. Din; racket; noise
5. Honest; direct
6. Animal kept for amusement or companionship
8. Person who gives medical care to animals
10. Place where grain is ground
13. Tightly stretched
14. Gentle push
15. Tired
17. Visual mark or sign
19. Highly sensitive to something physically
20. Rotting; decaying
22. Pity or sorrow for distress of another
25. Lost; wandering
26. Short, sharp bark or cry

Shiloh Vocabulary Crossword 1 Answer Key

	1 N		2 W	I	T	N	3 E	S	S			4 C
5 S	L	U	M	P			L					L
Q		M	7 E	8 N	V	Y	9 R	O	O	T	E	D	A
U		B	T	E		10 G		G				11 B	A	T	S
A				12 T	H	R	U	13 S	T	14 I	N	G
R			15 T			I		E		U		E
16 E	17 T	H	U	S	I	A	S	M		N	D	18 H	19 A	R	M
	R		C			T		S		G		L
	A		K	20 S		21 M	A	Z	E			L	22 S
	23 C	H	E	A	P	I						E	Y
	E		R	24 O	B	L	I	G	E	D	25 S	C	R	A	M
			E	I		L					T		G		P
			D	L		26 Y	A	N	K		R		I		A
				27 W	I	N	C	E			A		C		T
				N			28 L	O	N	E	L	Y			H
29 B	A	W	L	I	N	G		P							Y

Across
2. Someone who signs a document to make it authentic
5. Fall; sink; droop
7. Resentment caused by desire for another's possessions
9. Firmly established; set
11. Flutters
12. Shoving
16. Excitement or interest for or in something
18. Wrong
21. Network of interconnecting pathways
23. At low cost; inexpensive
24. Obligated; grateful
25. Get out; Go away
26. Pull with sudden force
27. Move involuntarily, as in pain
28. Sad at being alone
29. Sobbing loudly; crying; wailing

Down
1. Unable to feel normally
3. Walks in a slow, labored way
4. Din; racket; noise
5. Honest; direct
6. Animal kept for amusement or companionship
8. Person who gives medical care to animals
10. Place where grain is ground
13. Tightly stretched
14. Gentle push
15. Tired
17. Visual mark or sign
19. Highly sensitive to something physically
20. Rotting; decaying
22. Pity or sorrow for distress of another
25. Lost; wandering
26. Short, sharp bark or cry

Shiloh Vocabulary Crossword 2

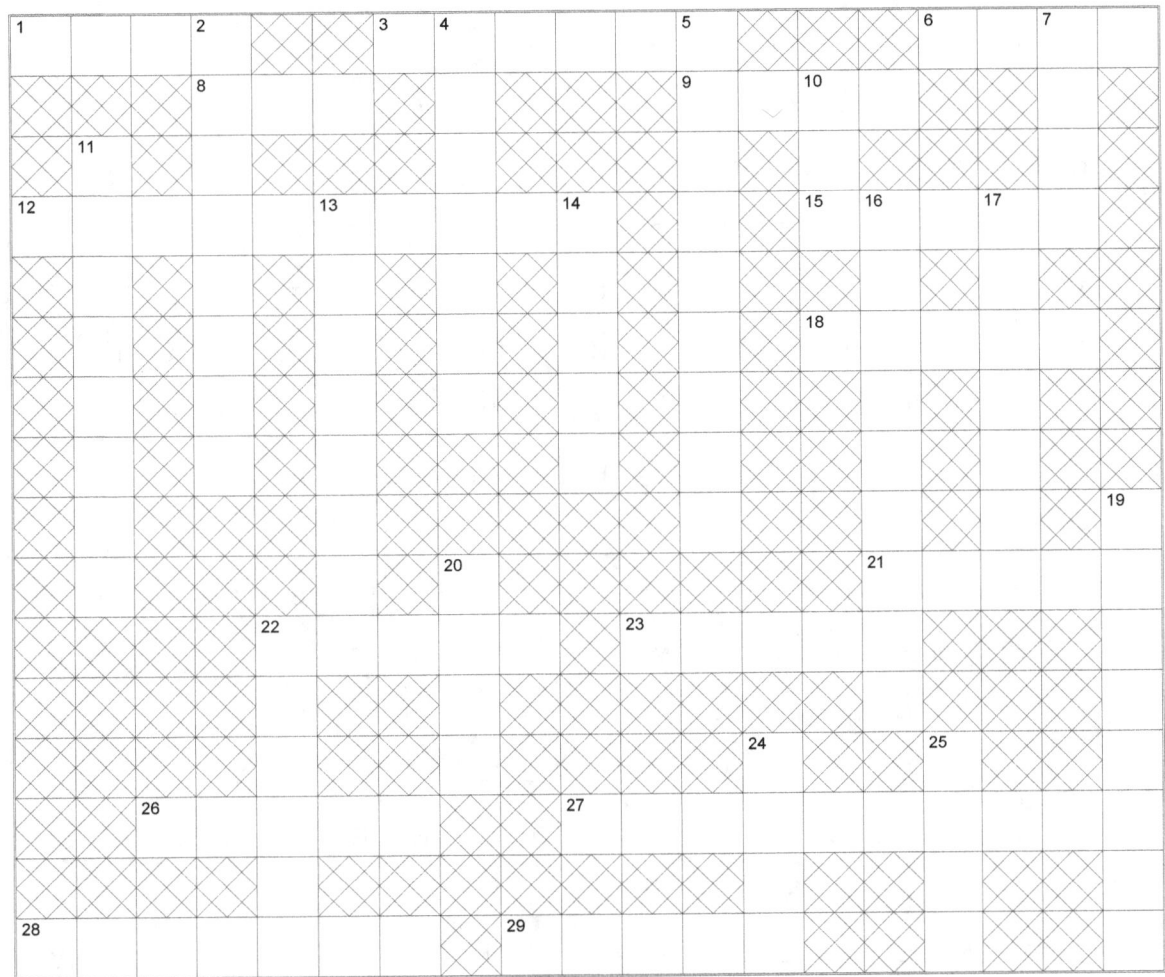

Across
1. Flutters
3. Firmly established; set
6. Unable to feel normally
8. Animal kept for amusement or companionship
9. Resentment caused by desire for another's possessions
12. A joyful celebration
15. Visual mark or sign
18. At low cost; inexpensive
21. Lost; wandering
22. Get out; Go away
23. Move involuntarily, as in pain
26. Small, chicken-like game bird
27. Acrobatic stunt in which the body rolls in a circle
28. Someone who signs a document to make it authentic
29. Fall; sink; droop

Down
2. Rotting; decaying
4. Obligated; grateful
5. Mischief; annoyance
7. Network of interconnecting pathways
10. Person who gives medical care to animals
11. Complete
13. Highly sensitive to something physically
14. Gentle push
16. Practiced
17. Din; racket; noise
19. Pity or sorrow for distress of another
20. Wrong
22. Honest; direct
24. Short, sharp bark or cry
25. Pull with sudden force

Shiloh Vocabulary Crossword 2 Answer Key

	1 B	A	T	2 S			3 R	4 O	O	T	E	5 D			6 N		7 U	M	B
				8 P	E	T		B				9 E	N	10 V	Y		A		
			11 O		O			L				V		E			Z		
12 J	U	B	I	L	A	13 T	I	O	14 N			I		15 T	16 R	A	17 C	E	
	T		L			L		G				L			E		L		
	R		I			L		E				M		18 C	H	E	A	P	
	I		N			E		D				E			E		T		
	G		G			R						N			A		T		
	H					G						T			R		E		19 S
	T					I		20 H						21 S	T	R	A	Y	
			22 S	C	R	A	M		23 W	I	N	C	E					M
			Q			R						D		25 Y				P	
			U			M			24 Y					Y				A	
		26 Q	U	A	I	L		27 S	O	M	E	R	S	A	U	L	T	
			R						L					N				H	
28 W	I	T	N	E	S	S		29 S	L	U	M	P		K				Y	

Across
1. Flutters
3. Firmly established; set
6. Unable to feel normally
8. Animal kept for amusement or companionship
9. Resentment caused by desire for another's possessions
12. A joyful celebration
15. Visual mark or sign
18. At low cost; inexpensive
21. Lost; wandering
22. Get out; Go away
23. Move involuntarily, as in pain
26. Small, chicken-like game bird
27. Acrobatic stunt in which the body rolls in a circle
28. Someone who signs a document to make it authentic
29. Fall; sink; droop

Down
2. Rotting; decaying
4. Obligated; grateful
5. Mischief; annoyance
7. Network of interconnecting pathways
10. Person who gives medical care to animals
11. Complete
13. Highly sensitive to something physically
14. Gentle push
16. Practiced
17. Din; racket; noise
19. Pity or sorrow for distress of another
20. Wrong
22. Honest; direct
24. Short, sharp bark or cry
25. Pull with sudden force

Shiloh Vocabulary Crossword 3

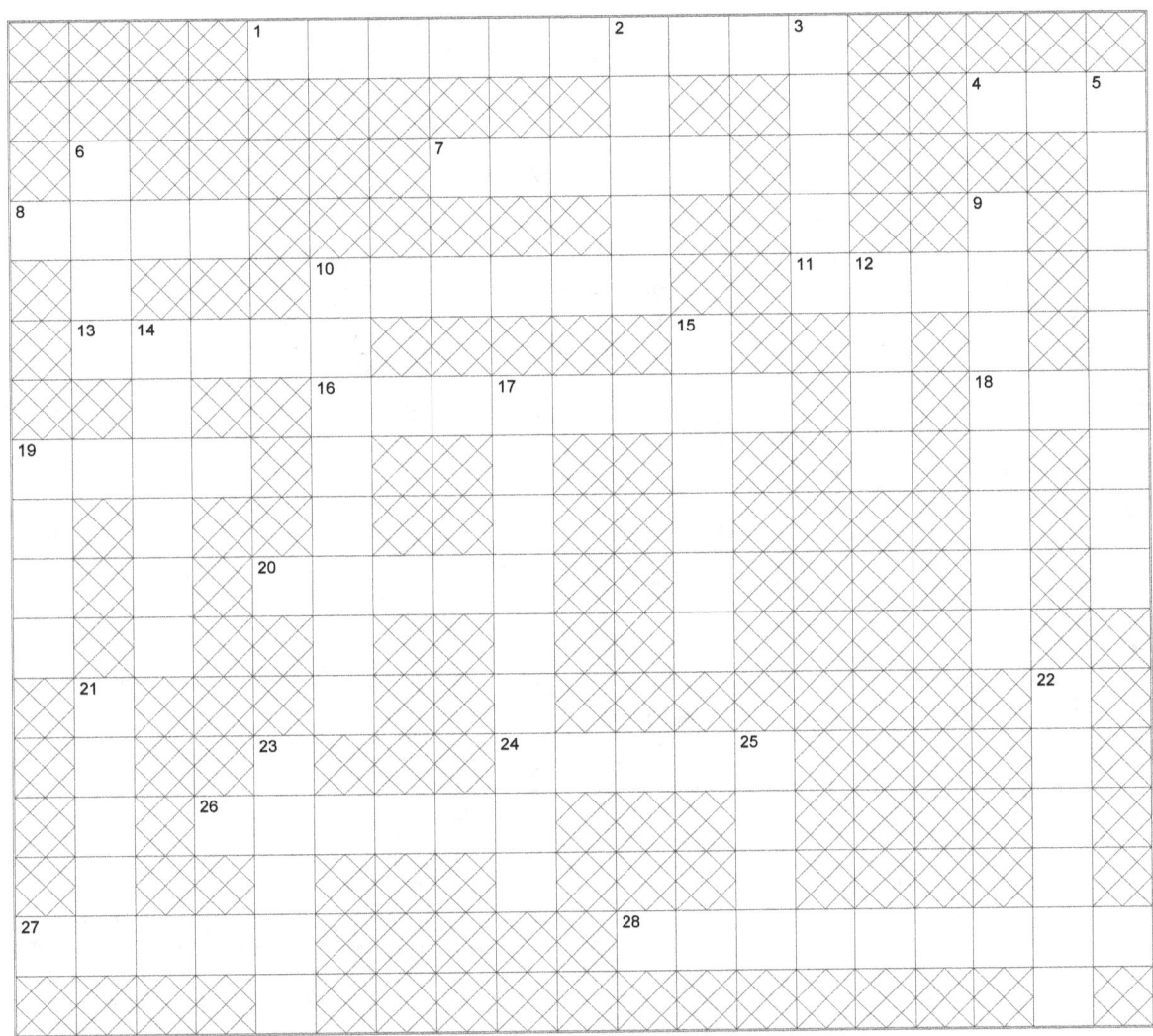

Across
1. A joyful celebration
4. Person who gives medical care to animals
7. Lost; wandering
8. Wrong
10. Honest; direct
11. Resentment caused by desire for another's possessions
13. Fall; sink; droop
16. Complete
18. Animal kept for amusement or companionship
19. Pull with sudden force
20. Move involuntarily, as in pain
24. Get out; Go away
26. Weak
27. Walks in a slow, labored way
28. Shaking from fear or excitement

Down
2. Visual mark or sign
3. Gentle push
5. Shoving
6. Flutters
9. Pity or sorrow for distress of another
10. Rotting; decaying
12. Unable to feel normally
14. Sad at being alone
15. Raises shoulders
17. Practiced
19. Short, sharp bark or cry
21. Small, chicken-like game bird
22. Running easily
23. Tightly stretched
25. Network of interconnecting pathways

Shiloh Vocabulary Crossword 3 Answer Key

			1 J	U	B	I	L	2 A	T	I	3 O	N			
								R			N			4 V	5 T
	6 B				7 S	T	R	A	Y		D			E	H
8 H	A	R	M					C			G		9 S		R
	T			10 S	Q	U	A	R	E		11 E	12 N	V	Y	U
	13 S	14 L	U	M	P				15 S		U		M		S
		O		16 O	U	17 T	R	I	G	H	T		18 P	E	T
19 Y	A	N	K		I		E		R			B	A		I
E		E			L		H		U				T		N
L		L		20 W	I	N	C	E					H		G
P		Y			N		A		S				Y		
	21 Q				G		R						22 L		
	U		23 T			24 S	C	R	A	25 M			O		
	A	26 F	E	E	B	L	E			A			P		
	I		N				D			Z			I		
27 S	L	O	G	S				28 T	R	E	M	B	L	I	N G
			E										N		G

Across
1. A joyful celebration
4. Person who gives medical care to animals
7. Lost; wandering
8. Wrong
10. Honest; direct
11. Resentment caused by desire for another's possessions
13. Fall; sink; droop
16. Complete
18. Animal kept for amusement or companionship
19. Pull with sudden force
20. Move involuntarily, as in pain
24. Get out; Go away
26. Weak
27. Walks in a slow, labored way
28. Shaking from fear or excitement

Down
2. Visual mark or sign
3. Gentle push
5. Shoving
6. Flutters
9. Pity or sorrow for distress of another
10. Rotting; decaying
12. Unable to feel normally
14. Sad at being alone
15. Raises shoulders
17. Practiced
19. Short, sharp bark or cry
21. Small, chicken-like game bird
22. Running easily
23. Tightly stretched
25. Network of interconnecting pathways

Shiloh Vocabulary Crossword 4

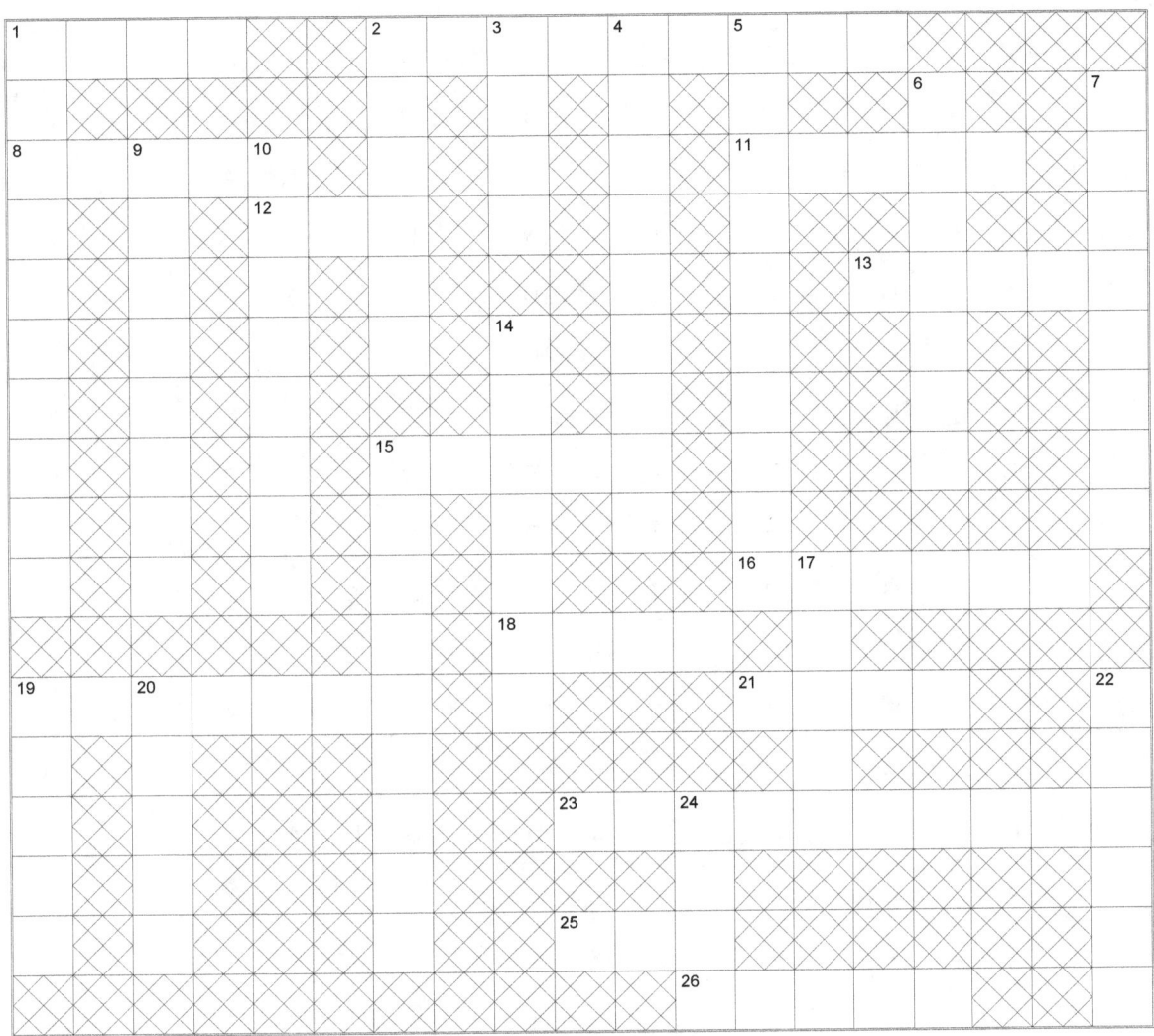

Across
1. Network of interconnecting pathways
2. Practiced
8. Walks in a slow, labored way
11. Lost; wandering
12. Animal kept for amusement or companionship
13. Fall; sink; droop
15. Visual mark or sign
16. Honest; direct
18. Resentment caused by desire for another's possessions
19. Someone who signs a document to make it authentic
21. Pull with sudden force
23. A joyful celebration
25. Person who gives medical care to animals
26. Get out; Go away

Down
1. Abused
2. Firmly established; set
3. Wrong
4. Deserted; forsaken
5. Hints; feelings of distrust
6. Sobbing loudly; crying; wailing
7. Pity or sorrow for distress of another
9. Complete
10. Rotting; decaying
14. Din; racket; noise
15. Shoving
17. Small, chicken-like game bird
19. Move involuntarily, as in pain
20. Tightly stretched
22. Sad at being alone
24. Flutters

Shiloh Vocabulary Crossword 4 Answer Key

	1 M	A	Z	E		2 R	3 E	H	4 A	5 R	S	E	D		
	I					O	A		B	U			6 B		7 S
	8 S	9 L	10 S			O	R		A	11 S	T	R	A	Y	Y
	T	U	12 P	E	T		M		N	P			W		M
	R	T	O		E				D	I		13 S	L	U	M P
	E	R	I		D		14 C		O	C			I		A
	A	I	L				L		N	I			N		T
	T	G	I		15 T	R	A	C	E				G		H
	E	H	N		H		T		D						Y
	D	T	G		R		T			16 S	17 Q	U	A	R	E
					U		18 E	N	V	Y		U			
19 W	20 T	I	T	N	E	S	S	R			21 Y	A	N	K	22 L
I	E						T				I				O
N	N					23 J	24 B	I	L	A	T	I	O	N
C	S						A								E
E	E				25 V	E	T							L
						26 S	C	R	A	M				Y

Across
1. Network of interconnecting pathways
2. Practiced
8. Walks in a slow, labored way
11. Lost; wandering
12. Animal kept for amusement or companionship
13. Fall; sink; droop
15. Visual mark or sign
16. Honest; direct
18. Resentment caused by desire for another's possessions
19. Someone who signs a document to make it authentic
21. Pull with sudden force
23. A joyful celebration
25. Person who gives medical care to animals
26. Get out; Go away

Down
1. Abused
2. Firmly established; set
3. Wrong
4. Deserted; forsaken
5. Hints; feelings of distrust
6. Sobbing loudly; crying; wailing
7. Pity or sorrow for distress of another
9. Complete
10. Rotting; decaying
14. Din; racket; noise
15. Shoving
17. Small, chicken-like game bird
19. Move involuntarily, as in pain
20. Tightly stretched
22. Sad at being alone
24. Flutters

Shiloh Vocabulary Juggle Letters 1

1. ERKUDECT = 1. _____
   Tired

2. CNIEW = 2. _____
   Move involuntarily, as in pain

3. BDLEGOI = 3. _____
   Obligated; grateful

4. EENST = 4. _____
   Tightly stretched

5. CITNIIOBSAT = 5. _____
   Substances used to treat infectious diseases

6. RSCAM = 6. _____
   Get out; Go away

7. VYNE = 7. _____
   Resentment caused by desire for another's possessions

8. UIAQL = 8. _____
   Small, chicken-like game bird

9. IGTURTSHN = 9. _____
   Shoving

10. BJNAOLTIUI =10. _____
    A joyful celebration

11. TOGHTRUI =11. _____
    Complete

12. MPDSUTE =12. _____
    Puzzled; baffled

13. NSAEHMISUT =13. _____
    Excitement or interest for or in something

14. OEDRTO =14. _____
    Firmly established; set

15. TVE =15. _____
    Person who gives medical care to animals

Shiloh Vocabulary Juggle Letters 1 Answer Key

1. ERKUDECT = 1. TUCKERED
   Tired
2. CNIEW = 2. WINCE
   Move involuntarily, as in pain
3. BDLEGOI = 3. OBLIGED
   Obligated; grateful
4. EENST = 4. TENSE
   Tightly stretched
5. CITNIIOBSAT = 5. ANTIBIOTICS
   Substances used to treat infectious diseases
6. RSCAM = 6. SCRAM
   Get out; Go away
7. VYNE = 7. ENVY
   Resentment caused by desire for another's possessions
8. UIAQL = 8. QUAIL
   Small, chicken-like game bird
9. IGTURTSHN = 9. THRUSTING
   Shoving
10. BJNAOLTIUI = 10. JUBILATION
    A joyful celebration
11. TOGHTRUI = 11. OUTRIGHT
    Complete
12. MPDSUTE = 12. STUMPED
    Puzzled; baffled
13. NSAEHMISUT = 13. ENTHUSIASM
    Excitement or interest for or in something
14. OEDRTO = 14. ROOTED
    Firmly established; set
15. TVE = 15. VET
    Person who gives medical care to animals

Shiloh Vocabulary Juggle Letters 2

1. ILINOGSP = 1. _____
   Rotting; decaying

2. GWLIABN = 2. _____
   Sobbing loudly; crying; wailing

3. SOPICUSSIN = 3. _____
   Hints; feelings of distrust

4. LACGRIEL = 4. _____
   Highly sensitive to something physically

5. BJIAONLTUI = 5. _____
   A joyful celebration

6. UMTESPD = 6. _____
   Puzzled; baffled

7. HSSUGR = 7. _____
   Raises shoulders

8. TSIWESN = 8. _____
   Someone who signs a document to make it authentic

9. ETIMTEDRAS = 9. _____
   Abused

10. OILGCDSN =10. _____
    Reprimanding; nagging

11. TBSA =11. _____
    Flutters

12. TEV =12. _____
    Person who gives medical care to animals

13. GERNILBTM =13. _____
    Shaking from fear or excitement

14. NTEES =14. _____
    Tightly stretched

15. ZGAGIGZNIG =15. _____
    Making a series of sharp turns

Shiloh Vocabulary Juggle Letters 2 Answer Key

1. ILINOGSP = 1. SPOILING
    Rotting; decaying

2. GWLIABN = 2. BAWLING
    Sobbing loudly; crying; wailing

3. SOPICUSSIN = 3. SUSPICIONS
    Hints; feelings of distrust

4. LACGRIEL = 4. ALLERGIC
    Highly sensitive to something physically

5. BJIAONLTUI = 5. JUBILATION
    A joyful celebration

6. UMTESPD = 6. STUMPED
    Puzzled; baffled

7. HSSUGR = 7. SHRUGS
    Raises shoulders

8. TSIWESN = 8. WITNESS
    Someone who signs a document to make it authentic

9. ETIMTEDRAS = 9. MISTREATED
    Abused

10. OILGCDSN = 10. SCOLDING
    Reprimanding; nagging

11. TBSA = 11. BATS
    Flutters

12. TEV = 12. VET
    Person who gives medical care to animals

13. GERNILBTM = 13. TREMBLING
    Shaking from fear or excitement

14. NTEES = 14. TENSE
    Tightly stretched

15. ZGAGIGZNIG = 15. ZIGZAGGING
    Making a series of sharp turns

Shiloh Vocabulary Juggle Letters 3

1. AHERREDES = 1. _____
   Practiced

2. EPT = 2. _____
   Animal kept for amusement or companionship

3. RTTACEL = 3. _____
   Din; racket; noise

4. URECEKDT = 4. _____
   Tired

5. EVT = 5. _____
   Person who gives medical care to animals

6. LWBGANI = 6. _____
   Sobbing loudly; crying; wailing

7. PHYMTYAS = 7. _____
   Pity or sorrow for distress of another

8. UGRSHS = 8. _____
   Raises shoulders

9. GGANIZGIZG = 9. _____
   Making a series of sharp turns

10. EINSTSW =10. _____
    Someone who signs a document to make it authentic

11. NYOLLE =11. _____
    Sad at being alone

12. EDUGN =12. _____
    Gentle push

13. EAPCH =13. _____
    At low cost; inexpensive

14. LBMCALKIA =14. _____
    Get by threatening

15. EVLEMNITD =15. _____
    Mischief; annoyance

Shiloh Vocabulary Juggle Letters 3 Answer Key

1. AHERREDES = 1. REHEARSED
   Practiced
2. EPT = 2. PET
   Animal kept for amusement or companionship
3. RTTACEL = 3. CLATTER
   Din; racket; noise
4. URECEKDT = 4. TUCKERED
   Tired
5. EVT = 5. VET
   Person who gives medical care to animals
6. LWBGANI = 6. BAWLING
   Sobbing loudly; crying; wailing
7. PHYMTYAS = 7. SYMPATHY
   Pity or sorrow for distress of another
8. UGRSHS = 8. SHRUGS
   Raises shoulders
9. GGANIZGIZG = 9. ZIGZAGGING
   Making a series of sharp turns
10. EINSTSW =10. WITNESS
    Someone who signs a document to make it authentic
11. NYOLLE =11. LONELY
    Sad at being alone
12. EDUGN =12. NUDGE
    Gentle push
13. EAPCH =13. CHEAP
    At low cost; inexpensive
14. LBMCALKIA =14. BLACKMAIL
    Get by threatening
15. EVLEMNITD =15. DEVILMENT
    Mischief; annoyance

Shiloh Vocabulary Juggle Letters 4

1. IIOSPNSSCU = 1. _____
   Hints; feelings of distrust

2. NYKA = 2. _____
   Pull with sudden force

3. IGNCLSDO = 3. _____
   Reprimanding; nagging

4. SRAMC = 4. _____
   Get out; Go away

5. TRATECL = 5. _____
   Din; racket; noise

6. STBA = 6. _____
   Flutters

7. ITMHESNSAU = 7. _____
   Excitement or interest for or in something

8. IBNAWGL = 8. _____
   Sobbing loudly; crying; wailing

9. GIOIAERTTSVN = 9. _____
   Person who inquires or examines

10. PCEAH =10. _____
    At low cost; inexpensive

11. OEDORT =11. _____
    Firmly established; set

12. ENGDU =12. _____
    Gentle push

13. NLPIOG =13. _____
    Running easily

14. LIAUQ =14. _____
    Small, chicken-like game bird

15. LSOESNDB =15. _____
    Fearlessness and daring

Shiloh Vocabulary Juggle Letters 4 Answer Key

1. IIOSPNSSCU = 1. SUSPICIONS
   Hints; feelings of distrust

2. NYKA = 2. YANK
   Pull with sudden force

3. IGNCLSDO = 3. SCOLDING
   Reprimanding; nagging

4. SRAMC = 4. SCRAM
   Get out; Go away

5. TRATECL = 5. CLATTER
   Din; racket; noise

6. STBA = 6. BATS
   Flutters

7. ITMHESNSAU = 7. ENTHUSIASM
   Excitement or interest for or in something

8. IBNAWGL = 8. BAWLING
   Sobbing loudly; crying; wailing

9. GIOIAERTTSVN = 9. INVESTIGATOR
   Person who inquires or examines

10. PCEAH = 10. CHEAP
    At low cost; inexpensive

11. OEDORT = 11. ROOTED
    Firmly established; set

12. ENGDU = 12. NUDGE
    Gentle push

13. NLPIOG = 13. LOPING
    Running easily

14. LIAUQ = 14. QUAIL
    Small, chicken-like game bird

15. LSOESNDB = 15. BOLDNESS
    Fearlessness and daring

ABANDONED	Deserted; forsaken
ALLERGIC	Highly sensitive to something physically
ANTIBIOTICS	Substances used to treat infectious diseases
BATS	Flutters
BAWLING	Sobbing loudly; crying; wailing
BLACKMAIL	Get by threatening

BOLDNESS	Fearlessness and daring
CHEAP	At low cost; inexpensive
CLATTER	Din; racket; noise
CLINKING	Making a light, sharp ringing sound
DEVILMENT	Mischief; annoyance
ENTHUSIASM	Excitement or interest for or in something

ENVY	Resentment caused by desire for another's possessions
FEEBLE	Weak
GRISTMILL	Place where grain is ground
GROVELING	Cringing
HARM	Wrong
INVESTIGATOR	Person who inquires or examines

JUBILATION	A joyful celebration
LONELY	Sad at being alone
LOPING	Running easily
MAZE	Network of interconnecting pathways
MISTREATED	Abused
NUDGE	Gentle push

NUMB	Unable to feel normally
OBLIGED	Obligated; grateful
OUTRIGHT	Complete
PET	Animal kept for amusement or companionship
QUAIL	Small, chicken-like game bird
REHEARSED	Practiced

ROOTED	Firmly established; set
SCOLDING	Reprimanding; nagging
SCRAM	Get out; Go away
SHRUGS	Raises shoulders
SLOGS	Walks in a slow, labored way
SLUMP	Fall; sink; droop

SOMERSAULT	Acrobatic stunt in which the body rolls in a circle
SPOILING	Rotting; decaying
SQUARE	Honest; direct
STRAY	Lost; wandering
STUMPED	Puzzled; baffled
SUSPICIONS	Hints; feelings of distrust

SYMPATHY	Pity or sorrow for distress of another
TENSE	Tightly stretched
THRUSTING	Shoving
TRACE	Visual mark or sign
TREMBLING	Shaking from fear or excitement
TUCKERED	Tired

VET	Person who gives medical care to animals
WINCE	Move involuntarily, as in pain
WITNESS	Someone who signs a document to make it authentic
YANK	Pull with sudden force
YELP	Short, sharp bark or cry
ZIGZAGGING	Making a series of sharp turns

Shiloh Vocabulary

STUMPED	STRAY	SHRUGS	JUBILATION	SLOGS
ZIGZAGGING	LONELY	GROVELING	REHEARSED	ALLERGIC
HARM	NUDGE	FREE SPACE	MISTREATED	TENSE
QUAIL	WITNESS	SCRAM	LOPING	VET
ANTIBIOTICS	WINCE	CLATTER	FEEBLE	NUMB

Shiloh Vocabulary

SLUMP	PET	ENVY	SYMPATHY	TRACE
BAWLING	TREMBLING	OBLIGED	SOMERSAULT	CHEAP
THRUSTING	ABANDONED	FREE SPACE	YANK	SUSPICIONS
DEVILMENT	INVESTIGATOR	BLACKMAIL	BOLDNESS	ROOTED
CLINKING	OUTRIGHT	YELP	SPOILING	GRISTMILL

Shiloh Vocabulary

TENSE	FEEBLE	ENTHUSIASM	TUCKERED	QUAIL
SOMERSAULT	LOPING	SPOILING	PET	DEVILMENT
SLUMP	ENVY	FREE SPACE	SCOLDING	BLACKMAIL
REHEARSED	STUMPED	MAZE	OBLIGED	BATS
CLINKING	ZIGZAGGING	SLOGS	YELP	ROOTED

Shiloh Vocabulary

MISTREATED	TREMBLING	NUMB	LONELY	JUBILATION
TRACE	ALLERGIC	GROVELING	CHEAP	BAWLING
CLATTER	GRISTMILL	FREE SPACE	STRAY	WINCE
OUTRIGHT	SHRUGS	THRUSTING	ANTIBIOTICS	SYMPATHY
NUDGE	VET	ABANDONED	SUSPICIONS	INVESTIGATOR

Shiloh Vocabulary

SHRUGS	OUTRIGHT	ENTHUSIASM	CHEAP	WITNESS
ALLERGIC	LOPING	HARM	REHEARSED	THRUSTING
TRACE	MISTREATED	FREE SPACE	SCOLDING	BAWLING
CLINKING	PET	NUMB	ROOTED	YELP
MAZE	BLACKMAIL	STUMPED	SQUARE	SLUMP

Shiloh Vocabulary

YANK	LONELY	WINCE	SYMPATHY	TREMBLING
VET	ENVY	SLOGS	GRISTMILL	SUSPICIONS
SPOILING	BOLDNESS	FREE SPACE	INVESTIGATOR	BATS
TUCKERED	TENSE	ZIGZAGGING	ABANDONED	SCRAM
QUAIL	DEVILMENT	ANTIBIOTICS	SOMERSAULT	JUBILATION

Shiloh Vocabulary

STRAY	NUMB	CLATTER	SPOILING	NUDGE
LONELY	SHRUGS	OBLIGED	ANTIBIOTICS	THRUSTING
SCRAM	VET	FREE SPACE	ENVY	SLOGS
SCOLDING	TREMBLING	YANK	SLUMP	ABANDONED
HARM	BOLDNESS	TUCKERED	QUAIL	OUTRIGHT

Shiloh Vocabulary

MAZE	ALLERGIC	CLINKING	GRISTMILL	WINCE
REHEARSED	JUBILATION	TENSE	YELP	DEVILMENT
LOPING	INVESTIGATOR	FREE SPACE	PET	ENTHUSIASM
BATS	GROVELING	WITNESS	MISTREATED	ROOTED
SUSPICIONS	FEEBLE	ZIGZAGGING	TRACE	BLACKMAIL

Shiloh Vocabulary

ALLERGIC	VET	ROOTED	TRACE	CLINKING
LONELY	MISTREATED	JUBILATION	INVESTIGATOR	HARM
REHEARSED	ABANDONED	FREE SPACE	CLATTER	TREMBLING
BAWLING	QUAIL	WINCE	CHEAP	GRISTMILL
SCRAM	YANK	SQUARE	ANTIBIOTICS	SUSPICIONS

Shiloh Vocabulary

PET	SYMPATHY	TUCKERED	YELP	WITNESS
OUTRIGHT	LOPING	TENSE	BATS	ZIGZAGGING
STRAY	NUMB	FREE SPACE	SOMERSAULT	SLOGS
DEVILMENT	OBLIGED	ENVY	FEEBLE	SPOILING
NUDGE	SLUMP	BLACKMAIL	STUMPED	THRUSTING

Shiloh Vocabulary

BLACKMAIL	SLOGS	OBLIGED	SPOILING	SYMPATHY
NUDGE	BATS	NUMB	ENTHUSIASM	LOPING
SCRAM	CLINKING	FREE SPACE	ENVY	TENSE
ANTIBIOTICS	PET	YELP	WITNESS	YANK
WINCE	STRAY	SOMERSAULT	ROOTED	CLATTER

Shiloh Vocabulary

QUAIL	ABANDONED	FEEBLE	GRISTMILL	ZIGZAGGING
SQUARE	MAZE	GROVELING	TUCKERED	SUSPICIONS
SHRUGS	THRUSTING	FREE SPACE	BOLDNESS	STUMPED
SLUMP	HARM	TREMBLING	VET	CHEAP
OUTRIGHT	TRACE	DEVILMENT	ALLERGIC	MISTREATED

Shiloh Vocabulary

TUCKERED	WINCE	SOMERSAULT	SUSPICIONS	CLATTER
ALLERGIC	TREMBLING	TRACE	FEEBLE	GRISTMILL
BOLDNESS	ZIGZAGGING	FREE SPACE	NUMB	CLINKING
QUAIL	SCRAM	OUTRIGHT	NUDGE	SQUARE
BAWLING	YANK	SCOLDING	STRAY	MISTREATED

Shiloh Vocabulary

JUBILATION	SLUMP	GROVELING	BLACKMAIL	THRUSTING
BATS	CHEAP	PET	OBLIGED	HARM
SHRUGS	MAZE	FREE SPACE	ENVY	SLOGS
VET	REHEARSED	ROOTED	YELP	INVESTIGATOR
SPOILING	WITNESS	DEVILMENT	LOPING	ENTHUSIASM

Shiloh Vocabulary

ZIGZAGGING	ROOTED	FEEBLE	TENSE	NUDGE
NUMB	TREMBLING	HARM	SPOILING	SCRAM
PET	BOLDNESS	FREE SPACE	MAZE	ENTHUSIASM
ENVY	TRACE	QUAIL	MISTREATED	YELP
SLUMP	CLATTER	SYMPATHY	LONELY	ABANDONED

Shiloh Vocabulary

WITNESS	DEVILMENT	SOMERSAULT	ALLERGIC	WINCE
OUTRIGHT	ANTIBIOTICS	THRUSTING	LOPING	JUBILATION
SCOLDING	SQUARE	FREE SPACE	SHRUGS	TUCKERED
INVESTIGATOR	BAWLING	BLACKMAIL	CHEAP	OBLIGED
YANK	BATS	GRISTMILL	REHEARSED	CLINKING

Shiloh Vocabulary

HARM	DEVILMENT	BAWLING	CHEAP	OUTRIGHT
STUMPED	ENTHUSIASM	BOLDNESS	YELP	ANTIBIOTICS
SLUMP	LONELY	FREE SPACE	OBLIGED	TENSE
THRUSTING	STRAY	GRISTMILL	MAZE	SHRUGS
BATS	ABANDONED	GROVELING	INVESTIGATOR	LOPING

Shiloh Vocabulary

NUMB	MISTREATED	TREMBLING	SYMPATHY	CLINKING
WINCE	ROOTED	ENVY	SQUARE	VET
ALLERGIC	SCRAM	FREE SPACE	REHEARSED	WITNESS
TUCKERED	PET	NUDGE	SUSPICIONS	TRACE
FEEBLE	YANK	SPOILING	SCOLDING	SOMERSAULT

Shiloh Vocabulary

SQUARE	CHEAP	SLOGS	YELP	GRISTMILL
ABANDONED	QUAIL	TUCKERED	YANK	ROOTED
ENTHUSIASM	HARM	FREE SPACE	OUTRIGHT	PET
CLATTER	ANTIBIOTICS	NUMB	SYMPATHY	WINCE
OBLIGED	FEEBLE	SUSPICIONS	SCOLDING	ZIGZAGGING

Shiloh Vocabulary

CLINKING	BOLDNESS	STRAY	INVESTIGATOR	TENSE
ALLERGIC	SOMERSAULT	SHRUGS	LOPING	THRUSTING
MAZE	MISTREATED	FREE SPACE	SCRAM	JUBILATION
VET	NUDGE	SPOILING	TREMBLING	SLUMP
BATS	STUMPED	REHEARSED	LONELY	BAWLING

Shiloh Vocabulary

CLINKING	SUSPICIONS	LOPING	SLOGS	SQUARE
YANK	NUMB	YELP	THRUSTING	INVESTIGATOR
WINCE	BAWLING	FREE SPACE	STUMPED	MAZE
ABANDONED	SPOILING	WITNESS	FEEBLE	BATS
JUBILATION	HARM	ZIGZAGGING	ENVY	SHRUGS

Shiloh Vocabulary

SCOLDING	LONELY	QUAIL	ANTIBIOTICS	ROOTED
NUDGE	BOLDNESS	PET	SLUMP	OUTRIGHT
OBLIGED	MISTREATED	FREE SPACE	REHEARSED	SCRAM
VET	GROVELING	STRAY	TUCKERED	SOMERSAULT
TENSE	ENTHUSIASM	DEVILMENT	GRISTMILL	TREMBLING

Shiloh Vocabulary

TRACE	CLINKING	VET	SLOGS	FEEBLE
YANK	CHEAP	NUMB	SHRUGS	WITNESS
MAZE	BATS	FREE SPACE	SYMPATHY	ROOTED
CLATTER	ANTIBIOTICS	SOMERSAULT	REHEARSED	MISTREATED
DEVILMENT	OBLIGED	HARM	SCRAM	SPOILING

Shiloh Vocabulary

GROVELING	SLUMP	LONELY	BAWLING	PET
OUTRIGHT	TENSE	WINCE	SQUARE	INVESTIGATOR
STRAY	BOLDNESS	FREE SPACE	ZIGZAGGING	ALLERGIC
STUMPED	LOPING	QUAIL	BLACKMAIL	ABANDONED
NUDGE	TUCKERED	GRISTMILL	SCOLDING	TREMBLING

Shiloh Vocabulary

ENVY	LONELY	ABANDONED	TRACE	INVESTIGATOR
CLINKING	ROOTED	REHEARSED	YANK	VET
OBLIGED	SQUARE	FREE SPACE	DEVILMENT	HARM
TREMBLING	OUTRIGHT	TENSE	JUBILATION	SCOLDING
CLATTER	WINCE	ZIGZAGGING	MISTREATED	SYMPATHY

Shiloh Vocabulary

SUSPICIONS	STRAY	NUDGE	ANTIBIOTICS	YELP
SHRUGS	PET	STUMPED	ENTHUSIASM	CHEAP
THRUSTING	GROVELING	FREE SPACE	SLUMP	NUMB
SLOGS	BATS	SOMERSAULT	QUAIL	BLACKMAIL
WITNESS	FEEBLE	ALLERGIC	SCRAM	LOPING

Shiloh Vocabulary

SUSPICIONS	ROOTED	INVESTIGATOR	STUMPED	OUTRIGHT
SCOLDING	SQUARE	MAZE	TREMBLING	SLOGS
SHRUGS	TRACE	FREE SPACE	LONELY	DEVILMENT
BOLDNESS	THRUSTING	SOMERSAULT	HARM	NUMB
ALLERGIC	BATS	NUDGE	CLINKING	CHEAP

Shiloh Vocabulary

GROVELING	ENVY	REHEARSED	CLATTER	OBLIGED
FEEBLE	STRAY	LOPING	WINCE	TENSE
PET	ANTIBIOTICS	FREE SPACE	BLACKMAIL	SYMPATHY
MISTREATED	BAWLING	GRISTMILL	WITNESS	SLUMP
ABANDONED	ZIGZAGGING	ENTHUSIASM	SCRAM	YANK

Shiloh Vocabulary

SLUMP	BAWLING	CLINKING	FEEBLE	SCOLDING
REHEARSED	NUMB	YANK	CLATTER	TENSE
SYMPATHY	ANTIBIOTICS	FREE SPACE	ABANDONED	OBLIGED
ZIGZAGGING	BATS	ENTHUSIASM	BOLDNESS	SHRUGS
DEVILMENT	LOPING	ALLERGIC	GRISTMILL	OUTRIGHT

Shiloh Vocabulary

TUCKERED	VET	WINCE	SPOILING	LONELY
BLACKMAIL	NUDGE	SLOGS	SOMERSAULT	YELP
HARM	JUBILATION	FREE SPACE	ENVY	SQUARE
STRAY	MAZE	MISTREATED	ROOTED	GROVELING
STUMPED	PET	CHEAP	QUAIL	SUSPICIONS

Shiloh Vocabulary

STRAY	LOPING	YANK	THRUSTING	TUCKERED
VET	SOMERSAULT	CHEAP	TREMBLING	SLUMP
SPOILING	BOLDNESS	FREE SPACE	SCOLDING	INVESTIGATOR
SQUARE	QUAIL	WINCE	BATS	YELP
REHEARSED	JUBILATION	ENVY	ZIGZAGGING	SHRUGS

Shiloh Vocabulary

DEVILMENT	ANTIBIOTICS	NUDGE	LONELY	CLINKING
TRACE	SLOGS	STUMPED	ROOTED	ENTHUSIASM
GROVELING	OBLIGED	FREE SPACE	SYMPATHY	GRISTMILL
ABANDONED	FEEBLE	BLACKMAIL	WITNESS	BAWLING
HARM	PET	ALLERGIC	NUMB	SCRAM